Presented To:

_____

From:

_____

Date:

_____

A Biblical Approach to
the Armour of God and Spiritual Warfare

Why

War

APMI Publications
a division of Kingdom Dimension Books
P.O. Box 17,
55051 Barga (LU),
Tuscany, Italy

Why War

DR. ALAN PATEMAN

BOOK TITLE:
Why War: A Biblical Approach to the Armour of God and Spiritual Warfare

This edition published in 2013

Published by APMI Publications
A Division of Kingdom Dimension Books, Library No. **11**
P.O. Box 17,
55051 Barga (LU),
Italy

Email: publications@alanpatemanworldmissions.com
www.AlanPatemanWorldMissions.com

**APMI Publications and Kingdom Dimension Books are a division of
Alan Pateman World Missions**

Printed in the United States of America, Europe and Asia

Paperback ISBN: 978-1-909132-39-9
Hardcover ISBN: 978-1-909132-95-5
eBook ISBN: 978-1-909132-38-2

Acknowledgements:
Author/Design/Senior Editor/Publisher: Apostle Dr. Alan Pateman
Editing/Proofreading/Research: Dr. Jennifer Pateman
Computer Administration/Office Manager: Dr. Dorothea Struhlik
Cover Image Credit: © Nejron Photo www.fotolia.com

*Unless otherwise indicated, all scriptural quotations are from the King James Version of the Bible. Where scriptures appear with special emphasis (**in bold**, italic or <u>underlined</u>) we have edited them ourselves in order to bring focused attention within the context of this subject being taught.*

❖

Dedication

*To my wife Jenny and our
three children, Andrew James,
Naomi and Abigail.*

❖

Acknowledgements

I want to thank all of my friends and colleagues who have endorsed this book by contributing to its publication. Your selfless support is truly admirable. I appreciate each and everyone of you, your families, ministries and churches.

Apostle Benjamin Ayim Asare
Followers of Christ Int. Church
Novara, Italy
bayimasare@yahoo.it
www.benjaminayimasareministries.com

Pastors Dr. Tony & Josie Botfield
Oasis Christian Fellowship Telford
Telford, United Kingdom
ukdirector@alanpateman.com
www.oasischristianfellowshiptelford.com

Pastor Isaac Edomwonyi
Christ Intervention Ministries
Pistoia, Italy
epastorisaac@yahoo.com

Apostle Tom Hayden
Breakthrough Worship Centere'
Dunedin, Florida, USA
prophetom@mac.com
www.breakthroughworshipcentere.com

Elder Godson Chikezie Ibeh
Followers of Christ Int. Church
Novara, Italy
ibesons234@yahoo.com
www.focicnova.com

Rev. Blessing Ogbonmwan
European Coordinator: Christ Apostolic Church of God Mission
Merksem, Antwerp, Belgium
cacgmbelgiumparish@yahoo.com
www.cacgmfaithworkscenter.org

Apostle John Osborne
Now Revival Ministries
London, United Kingdom
infonowrevivalministries@yahoo.com

Alan Jr and Rebecca Pateman
Kingdom Expanse
Bückeburg, Germany
media@kingdomexpanse.com
www.kingdomexpanse.com

Pastor Edmund Sackey
Lighthouse International Christian Fellowship, House of Solution
Mülheim an der Ruhr, Germany
pastoredmund@houseofsolution.org
www.houseofsolution.net

Apostle Susan
Kingdom Life Center (KLC)
Antwerp, Belgium
klc.bel@gmail.com

Rev. Dr. Ralph N. Tioni
International Restoration Missionary Ministries
Düsseldorf, Germany
dr.ralphnjawe@ymail.com
www.irmm.bplaced.net

Pastor David Quarshie
Christian Praise Int. Centre
Boves, Italy
davidquarshie2007@yahoo.it

❖

Table of Contents

	Introduction	15
Chapter 1	The Full Armour of God	19
Chapter 2	Everything Hinges on the Loinbelt	27
Chapter 3	The Breastplate of Covering Righteousness	35
Chapter 4	Footwear of Readiness	43
Chapter 5	Carriers of Peace	55
Chapter 6	Formidable Shield of Faith	69
Chapter 7	The Helmet of Salvation	79

Chapter 8   The Sword that the Spirit Wields..............93

Chapter 9   Our Far Reaching Prayer Lance.............103

Chapter 10   Exalting the Name & The Blood............113

Chapter 11   Equipped with Power.............................123

Chapter 12   Forgiveness The Key to Revival............143

❖

Introduction

Jesus said, *"I saw Satan falling like a lightening [flash] from heaven. Behold!* **I have given you authority and power** *to trample upon serpents and scorpions… OVER ALL THE POWER THAT THE ENEMY POSSESSES and nothing shall in any way harm you. Nevertheless, do not rejoice at this, that* **the spirits are subject to you,** *but rejoice that your names are enrolled in heaven"* (Luke 10:18-20 AMP).

Spiritual warfare means different things to different people, but from a biblical standpoint Ephesians 6:10-18 gives us the best biblical definition of spiritual warfare possible. Arguably the objective of spiritual warfare is our minds, because as our minds are affected, so goes the rest of us *(individually and corporately)*. Entire families, companies and nations are effective or ineffective, depending on the mental stability of its people!

As believers we have been given the mind of Christ, yet we must understand that *EVERYTHING* seeks to prevent us from walking in such revelation knowledge. Describing this struggle exactly is 2 Corinthians 10:5 and yet I have to say that spiritual warfare is not just a *"mental"* struggle. Equally the *"full armour of God"* does not just consist of the *"helmet of salvation."*

Nevertheless the battlefield is usually staged in our minds before it progresses elsewhere. We are targeted in the arena of our mind, will and emotions, because it is easier to wear us down that way. Deceptions and delusions are absorbed by our minds in order for strongholds to be developed there and the consequences to be felt throughout the rest of our lives.

However God has designed it that we live in victory - spirit, soul and body - to enjoy an abundant life! For this God has thoroughly armed us, so that we can enforce the victory of Calvary that already defeated Satan. We must therefore no longer succumb to oppression and domination but put on the *"full armour of God"* so that we are ready to *"please him who hath chosen us to be soldiers"* (2 Timothy 2:4).

Finally in Acts 10:38 it tells us that Jesus went about doing good and healing *"all"* who were *"harassed and oppressed"* of the devil (AMP). Spiritual warfare then, is not just about self-defence. It includes helping others to overcome and to make way for Jesus in their lives. **THE KING Who has,** *"All authority (all power of rule) in heaven and on earth!"* (Matthew 28:18 AMP)

CHAPTER 1

The Full Armour of God

Gratefully we have not been *undone* before our enemy. Rather than stand naked and unclothed - God has more than adequately provided. Our spiritual clothing *IS* our arsenal!

"The full armour of God," has the capacity to foil the plans of each and every unseen force (*that has, is or ever will be*) organized against us.

Fully equipped - whom shall we fear? The only qualification or prerequisite necessary, is that we obediently, *"PUT IT ON!"*

> *Finally, be strong in the Lord and in his mighty power.* **PUT ON the full armour of God** *so that you can take your stand against the devil's schemes. For our struggle is not against flesh and blood, but against the rulers, against the authorities, against the powers of this dark world and against the spiritual forces of evil in the heavenly realms.*
>
> *Therefore* **PUT ON the full armour of God,** *so that when the day of evil comes, you may be able to* **stand your ground***, and after you have done everything,* **to stand. Stand firm** *then, with the belt of truth buckled around your waist, with the breastplate of righteousness in place, and with your feet fitted with the readiness that comes from the gospel of peace.*
>
> *In addition to all this,* **TAKE UP** *the shield of faith, with which you can extinguish all the flaming arrows of the evil one. Take the helmet of salvation and the sword of the Spirit, which is the Word of God. And pray in the Spirit on all occasions with all kinds of prayers and requests. With this in mind, be alert and always* **keep on praying for all the saints.**
>
> *(Ephesians 6:10-18)*

In Ephesians 6:10-18, Paul deals with key elements of spiritual warfare that we need to know and appropriate in our personal lives. In this book *"Why War?"* we will examine the specific pieces of armour that God has given to the Church, discovering its purpose and *practical application* in our *EVERYDAY LIVES.*

Straight Talk

However right at the onset here, I want to make something very plain; that spiritual warfare is not a religious ritual or an *extreme* that we visit. Nor is it just another doctrine or theology to divide us.

An emphasis on spiritual warfare is NOT the answer to our sin or to dealing with the negatives in our lives. Nor is warfare the answer to more provision, especially when we are in disobedience! Equally spiritual warfare is not the answer to a lack of discernment or the spiritual climate that we find ourselves in.

Instead we must at all times ensure that we have a day-to-day relationship *(experience)* with God that is found through intimacy, in the presence *(indwelling)* of His Holy Spirit. Offence is a barrier to His presence! Worship is an expression of our intimacy - loving Jesus first - then everything will follow... "it's all about Him!" One encounter with God's love will set you free.

Hardness of the heart, lack of love and critical judgments *(that only perceive the negatives)* are symptomatic or indicative of a wrong theology that's based only on *LAW.*

> *The fruit of the [Holy] Spirit [the work which His <u>presence</u> within accomplishes]...* ***against such things there is no law*** *[that can bring a charge].*
>
> (Galatians 5:22-23 AMP)

Remain Dove Minded

"The dove is clean by nature - so symbolizing the Holy Spirit. Solomon sings of His bride, *'My dove, my undefiled'* (Song of Solomon 6:9). In the Old Testament the dove is signified as being one of the clean birds for sacrifices. See how it is illustrated when Noah sent it forth from the ark. He first sent forth a raven, which failed to return; for it could land on carrion, a floating bloated corpse, or filth, but the dove, finding no clean place, returned.

'Though ye have lien with the pots, yet shall ye be as the wings of a dove, covered with silver, and her feathers with yellow gold' (Psalm 68:13). Here is the remarkable quality of the snow-white dove, to be around filth yet never partake of it; its snow-white feathers remain purely white. Do not expect the Holy Spirit to live in a filthy room, cob-webs, spiders, rats, bats, thick smoldering dust, odors, and filth everywhere. He is the pure dove, the Holy Spirit. He seeks our cleansing from all 'filthiness of the flesh and spirit.'

The dove is gentle by nature. When Christ sent forth His disciples, He told them to be *'harmless as doves'* (Matthew 10:16). The only reason given in the old times for the gentle disposition of the dove was, 'the dove has no gall.' The meat of an animal is ruined, if in cleaning it, the gall is broken. So the Holy Spirit is never spoken of as angry; **we have the wrath of the Lamb and of Almighty God, but never of the Spirit.** He can be grieved but never angered.

'The fruit of the Spirit is gentleness' (Galatians 5:21). The dove will not fight or strive, but can be rebuffed and many

times pine away. God's infinite Spirit will not force any doors, but would plead, and woo them to open. Be careful how you treat this Gentle Heavenly Dove. He will not break open any closed doors, nor carry them by storm; but He will send forth the fragrance of His presence to whisper to your heart what He can do for you.

The dove is by nature a lover. It is constant in its love. *'His eyes are as the eyes of the doves beside the rivers of waters'* (Song of Solomon 5:12). This is the constant love of Christ our heavenly Bridegroom Who can't get His eyes off us; so also is the Holy Spirit, *'Who loveth us to jealous envy.'* By nature the dove is a monogamist, mating but once and is true to that one through life. The Holy Spirit is the One *'Who sheds abroad the love of God in our hearts'"* [Bragg, p15].

Deliverance is Always God's Judgment

One question that must be addressed is the following: *"When negatives exist in life, is this due to God's judgment or is it just a consequence of fallen human nature?"* There is only one answer to this: **God's judgment is always deliverance.**

It is our job however to bring the reality of God's Kingdom to earth, *"…just as it is in heaven."*

> *As you go, preach…* **the kingdom of heaven is at hand! Cure the sick, raise the dead, cleanse the lepers, drive out demons.** *Freely (without pay) you have received, freely (without charge) give.*
>
> (Matthew 10:7-8 AMP)

By Their Fruits You Will Recognise Them

It's the presence & fruit of God's Holy Spirit in our lives that makes us recognisable (Matthew 7:20; Acts 19:15).

*The grace (favour and spiritual blessing) of the Lord Jesus Christ and the love of God and the **presence and fellowship (the communion and sharing together, and participation) in the Holy Spirit** be with you all. Amen (so be it).*

(2 Corinthians 13:14 AMP)

In a book like this we discover that we have been totally dressed and equipped for ACTION NOT PASSIVITY! However - I am still duty bound to ensure that my readers discern the importance of such chief elements that must never be missing from our spiritual walk regardless of the topic being studied:

- **Love:**
  (That none should Perish - John 3:16)

- **Presence:**
  (Partnership with the Holy Spirit)

- **Commission:**
  (To reveal His Kingdom to a fallen Humanity)

Operating From a Position of Victory

As the Body of Christ, we come from a position of victory and not defeat. We are *ACTIVE*. The Bride of Christ takes her place *(responsibility)* and does not adopt a *RESCUE ME* mentality. She knows that Christ has rescued her *(salvation)*. Now it's time to believe and act upon that salvation.

Likewise a marriage is about love first *(not selfishness because that's a form of control)*. Our salvation is secure and our relationship with Christ must be one of LOVE *(not obligation)*.

> *Therefore I tell you, her sins, many [as they are], are forgiven her - **because** **she has LOVED much**...*
>
> *(Luke 7:47 AMP)*

Our motive must be love and forgiveness *(see chapter 12)*, our mentality as a Body must not be negative. Even though discernment often reveals negatives, we must not adopt a judgmental attitude that opens the door for the devil - who is a consummate *"legalist"* and will always hold us to the law, which gives him the leverage to make claims and accusations against us (Revelation 12:10).

> *Do not judge, or you too will be judged. For in the same way you judge others, you will be judged, and **with the measure you use, it will be measured to you**.*
>
> *(Matthew 7:1-2 NIV)*

Nothing Replaces God's Presence

"Why War?" - is a valid question - yet this does not necessitate an over-indulgence in our mentality. In other words, **we must not become more aware of warfare than of God's Presence.** According to Ecclesiastes 3:8 there's *"...a time for war,"* but **there is never a time to relent away from the presence of God!**

> *Create in me a clean heart, O God, and renew a right, persevering, and steadfast spirit within me. **Cast me not***

*away from Your presence and take not Your Holy
Spirit from me.*

(Psalm 51:10-11 AMP)

We must not be drawn into anything that will take our
eyes off of Christ and His hard-won-victory *(this would always
be deception)*. Anything we do must be done in partnership-
with-God. That means we do EVERYTHING with Him and
NOTHING without Him. It's that simple!

This requires fresh daily *"revelation,"* so that we don't
walk or act in ignorance. Babies cannot go to war; but who
remains a baby? There is a huge difference between being
childish and childlike! God does not just require sincerity
but obedience. This requires growth. God wants us to mature
steadily *(without which every lesson we learn is a waste)*.

This veritable *"road-to-maturity"* is strewn with copious
responsibility but none greater than our daily relationship
with the Lord Jesus Christ. If we lose sight of this, we have
lost *everything*.

**Nevertheless it is OBEDIENCE that keeps our
relationship with Christ** *responsible* **and not just** *emotional!*
**And it is ACTION that keeps our faith out of the realm
of** *dead things* **and our devotion from being** *exclusively
pseudo!* (James 2:20,26)

❖

CHAPTER 2

Everything Hinges
on the Loinbelt

Something that we must comprehend right from the outset is that we have plainly been *outfitted for combat!* In Ephesians chapter 6, Paul was clearly not describing snorkelling equipment or beach wear. No! He was relating to the Roman soldier's equipment - to his full suit of ARMOUR. All the indication and evidence we need, to know that we are facing a very real spiritual battle, not a party nor a holiday. God Himself has essentially equipped us - for success - in *BATTLE!*

> **Stand firm** then, with the **belt of truth** buckled around your waist.
>
> *(Ephesians 6:14a)*

Although Jesus won the war - we still have many daily battles to face and this spiritual warfare that Ephesians is referring to, is no game. It is more real than we figure. In Ezekiel 21:31 God spoke of *"brutish men... skillful to destroy."* This describes the nature of a soldier; trained for armed combat, equal to a *skillful-killing-machine.* Some realities we like to ignore but war is always brutish and always produces casualties.

Even though he's a *defeated* foe, Satan still *plays-for-keeps,* luring as many lost souls as possible. By so doing, striking at the very heart of God who desires that, *"none should perish"* (John 3:16).

Paul instructed us to put on the full armour of God knowing full well that any soldier attempting to conduct warfare without it was doomed. Now Paul fashioned his suit of armour mentioned in Ephesians, on the soldier of his day - the Roman soldier.

The Loinbelt of Truth

To begin with I want to start by describing, what in my opinion, is the most crucial part of the soldier's outfit simply because so many other pieces of weaponry were connected to it - the *"loinbelt"* or more simply *"the belt of truth."*

However I want to stick with the "loinbelt" because in Shakespeare's poetic English, the loins traditionally referred to the source of a person's procreative power, the place where children come from! For example: *"He felt a stirring in his loins!"* It was considered the centre of man's being, his core! I like the fact that this is exactly where the truth is placed, right at our core.

So firstly connected to the *loin*-belt would have been the Roman soldier's large and considerably heavy shield *(not unlike an ordinary house hold door!)* that rested on a clip that was attached to the side of his loinbelt.

Then followed his two-edged sword that dangled at his side in a sheath that was also attached to the loinbelt. All in all this loinbelt was a vital piece of equipment!

The loinbelt was also needed to hold the breastplate together. Which comprised of two pieces of metal, held together at the waist by none other than the loinbelt. So quite simply if the Roman soldier had gone to battle without wearing his loinbelt - how disastrous this would have been - he would literally have come undone! Piece by piece, he would have fallen apart.

Once again the loinbelt was fixed around the soldiers waste, at the *core* of his being. At the very centre of who he was.

Cast not away therefore your confidence, which hath great recompense of reward.

(Hebrews 10:35)

The loinbelt offered the Roman soldier great confidence during battle. Assuring each pieces of his equipment would remain in place, releasing him to move swiftly and do combat without any entangling restrictions.

*No man that warreth **entangleth himself** with the affairs of this life; that he may please him who hath chosen him to be a soldier.*

(2 Timothy 2:4)

The Tangible Logos

The loinbelt of truth refers to the written Word of God. The Logos. A spiritual weapon that is tangible and in our physical hands! Above all and at the centre of everything rests the written Word of God; it is the most important piece of weaponry that we posses. Almost completely hidden by all the other pieces of equipment and smaller in size, yet most vital!

Clearly the results of neglecting our "loinbelt of truth" would be significant, such as becoming gradually insensitive to righteousness and peace. The gradual loss of joy *(in salvation)* and faith, quickly becoming dull and influenced heavily by unbelief.

Without the Word of God playing a dominant role in our lives, we simply cannot function. All our other abilities begin to wane and spiritual death takes place.

Removing the loinbelt - *the written Word of God* - from our lives causes us to fall apart piece by piece! Diabolical activity begins penetrating our usually protective insulation and confusion arises to take control.

The Roman soldier used to tuck up his tunic into his belt and it was the *first* piece of armour he would put on. Again it helped him move and fight untangled. *"Tuck up your tunic"* or *"Gird up your loins,"* means get ready for action! In Exodus 12:11 they also had to be fully dressed and ready to move. *(See also Luke 12:35 - switched on and ready to go!)*

In 1 Peter 1:13 it talks about girding up the *loins* of our *minds,* which is synonymous with preparing them to be ready and unhindered for action. I like the Message Bible's take on this particular verse:

> *So roll up your sleeves,* **put your mind in gear,** *be totally ready to receive the gift that's coming when Jesus arrives.*
> *(1 Peter 1:13 MSG)*

Paul clearly states that our loins must be *"girt about with truth."* Our belt therefore unmistakably refers to God's truth, which must be applied by the individual.

Speed is essential in battle and amongst other things, the loinbelt was designed to free-up soldiers to help make them swifter: *"...**his Word runneth very swiftly**"* (Psalms 147:15). Equally the TRUTH will give us the speed advantage over our enemy *(but only if applied!)*

Only Godly Character Can Wear
the Full Armour of God

Putting on God's truth has many practical implications for the Christian, in particular a life-style that reveals His truth and *a character that corresponds with His Word* (Ephesians 4:22-24).

Obviously this requires knowing God's Word and a willingness to live it out and act accordingly (1 John 5:2). Consider it like this: **character is what wears the armour!** The full armour of God is spiritual and must not be empty on the inside. A solider void of character, is a trained killing machine, ready to go AWOL. So Godly character is *everything* to the Christian and what makes us recognisable as God's own.

Godly character then, is also part of our arsenal, helping to hold up the armour from the inside out and give us the upper hand when it comes to our adversary. This is seen nowhere better than in Galatians chapter 5:18,23 where it says, *"If ye be led of the Spirit, ye are not under the law... against such there is no law."*

When we live both *yielded and obedient to* the fruits of the Holy Spirit, there can be no law levelled against us. Living above reproach is all about godly behaviour making it impossible, for accusation to stick!

The Accuser Searches for Falsehood

Satan is the *"accuser of our brethren... which accused them before our God day and night"* yet he finds it incredibly hard to bring accusations against Spirit led and obedient Christians. I did not say *"perfect Christians!"* but Spirit led and obedient Christians who essentially have no *falsehood* in them.

Satan tried to *find* something to accuse Jesus of, only to discover that He *"...did no sin, neither was **guile found** in his mouth"* (1 Peter 2:22, see also 1 Peter 3:10; Revelation 14:5;

John 1:47). To say that no guile was *"found"* in Jesus meant that someone had been looking! Yet Jesus was *"found"* 100% empty of guile.

In the Greek language *"guile"* refers to: *a decoy, a trick (bait),* **wile:-** *craft, deceit, and subtlety (see Strong's #1388).* Equally we must be found with no *"guile"* or **"wile"** *(trickery or deceit);* only Christ-like character.

Satan specializes and capitalizes on such **wiles.** *"Put on the whole armour of God, <u>that ye may be able</u> to stand against the* **wiles** *of the devil."* In fact this is the precise reason we have been so amply armed in the first place!

> *I will not talk with you much more, for the prince (evil genius, ruler) of the world is coming. And* **he has no claim on Me. [He has <u>nothing in common</u> with Me; there is nothing in Me that belongs to him,** *and he has no power over Me].*
>
> *(John 14:30 AMP)*

So when the devil comes looking, will he find guile in us? Will he find any **common ground?** Once again, character as much as any other weaponry that we possess, helps us to *overcome* the evil one - *on a daily basis.*

To end this particular chapter I want to quote from Rick Renner. As someone who is widely travelled myself, I can verify the following observations and affirm the fact that we cannot adopt any form of *"replacement theology."* Nothing can *"replace"* TRUTH in our lives. Not culture, not tradition, not methods or good ideas. Undeniably everything has its place, but without the truth playing its centre-role at the core - we inevitably come undone!

"God has allowed me to minister in thousands of church services over the years. As we have travelled, we have made several observations.

- **Praise and Worship are NOT the loinbelt:**
  Some ministers have tried to build their churches on praise and worship. Praise and worship are wonderful, but a person cannot build a church on this alone. Praise and worship are not the loinbelt!

- **Social Gatherings are NOT the loinbelt:**
  Others have tried to build churches on social gatherings. Times of fun and fellowship are good and needed in the local church, but a person cannot build a church on the foundation of social gatherings. Social gatherings and church fellowships are NOT the loinbelt!

- **Prayer is NOT the loinbelt:**
  Finally others have attempted to build their church entirely on prayer. Of course, prayer is vital. We have desperately needed a new emphasis on prayer in our day, but prayer is not the loinbelt! **Only the loinbelt will hold everything together for us, both as individual believers and as the corporate Body of Christ"** [Renner, p266].

❖

CHAPTER 3

The Breastplate of Covering Righteousness

It is a fact that the Roman soldiers used numerous types of breastplates, but one in particular was very ornate in nature and not used in war at all - only for ceremonial purposes.

In battle this ornate kind of breastplate would have served no purpose at all. Likewise we must ensure that we are using the right equipment at the right time and not just reaching each time for the - cosmetic and the shallow - especially when going into battle! *(A lack of basic revelation concerning the full armour of God, will incur in unnecessary casualties).*

> **To everything there is a season, and a time for every matter or purpose under heaven…** *a time to love and a time to hate,* **a time for war and a time for peace.**
> *(Ecclesiastes 3:1,8 AMP)*

So there is a time for *everything*. Even ceremonies have their place in the army. But when it counts the most, we aught to know what weapon is needed at the right moment! All soldiers require training and skill, to be able to recognise what is needed at the right time.

Just like Jesus knew exactly what scripture to use when facing Satan in the wilderness. At the height of spiritual battle *(and extreme physical weakness)*, He was yet able to discern and rightly divide the Word of truth, allowing it to have *maximum* effect! (2 Timothy 2:15)

> *Then Jesus said to him,* **Begone, Satan! For it has been written,** *You shall worship the Lord your God, and Him alone shall you serve.* **Then the devil departed from Him, and behold, angels came and ministered to Him.**
> *(Matthew 4:10 AMP)*

Returning to the breastplate, the Roman solider was in dire need for something to utterly cover and protect his vital organs against every method of attack; formidable and yet able to afford him full freedom of movement - while in the same token, able to hold up under pressure and daily wear and tare!

Stand firm then, with the belt of truth buckled around your waist, **with the breastplate of righteousness in place.**

(*Ephesians 6:14*)

The breastplate of the Roman soldier was probably the most glamorous piece of equipment the Roman soldier wore. Over and above his loinbelt and all other pieces of equipment, the breastplate was the most *attractive*.

Beginning at the top of the neck, it covered the soldier almost to his knees. Made of two different sides of metal, one for the front of the soldier and the other for the rare. The two sides of metal were held together at the top by metal rings, which were not visible and yet totally crucial in holding the breastplate together as one unit.

This piece of weaponry was also probably the heaviest that the soldier wore. At times could weigh in at well over 40 pounds/18 kilograms (*others reported to have weighed 75 pounds/34 kilograms or more, not forgetting Goliath's that weighed an incredible 125 pounds/57 kilograms - approximately!*)

Made of highly polished metal or brass the Roman soldier's breastplate could catch the sun's reflection, while marching (*at the right time of day*) creating a blinding effect for his enemy. Equally we must radiate the brilliance and glory of the Lord, in order to dazzle and strike fear into the heart of our adversaries!

Confidently Guarding the Heart

Protecting his vital organs, his breastplate offered the Roman soldier substantial protection and maximum *assurance* in battle. Likewise if anything can knock our confidence in battle - by making us overly self-conscious - we almost always become *ineffective* and easy targets. In fact anything that makes us focus on ourselves too much, is almost always deception!

One of the major organs that the breastplate protects is the heart, which according to scripture requires *maximum* protection *"**Above all else, guard your heart...**"* (Proverbs 4:23) *(When scripture says "above all else" we can safely assume that it's relatively important!)*

> ***Above all,*** *taking the shield of faith, wherewith ye shall be **able to quench all** the fiery darts of the wicked.*
> *(Ephesians 6:16)*

The Amplified Bible says, *"Lift up over all the [covering] shield of saving faith..."* simply because the correct context here is *position* not importance. In other words the shield of faith is not *more important* than any of the other weapons, but should just be held up to *"cover"* everything else - during battle! So it has a *"covering"* role, but not necessarily the *most* vital role.

However it's certain that while dressed in this *"full armour of God,"* we can enjoy **incredible capabilities**. Such as: *"...able to quench all"* - what an absolute! There is no failure in the word *"all."* So even though our enemy continuously fires arrows of criticism, insults, accusations, condemnation, loneliness, pride and much more, we are *"able"* to douse the lot *(but more about that later!)*

Righteousness that Covers

The righteousness of God which comes by believing with personal trust and confident reliance on Jesus Christ (the Messiah). [And it is meant] for all who believe. For there is no distinction...

(Romans 3:22 AMP)

Only when we are covered by God's righteousness *(not our own filthy rags)* can we enjoy perfect protection - through Jesus Christ. Whose redemptive work on the cross, made God's righteousness available to all - who believe - without segregation.

*Having predestinated us unto the **adoption of children by Jesus Christ to himself**... **In whom we have redemption through his blood**, the forgiveness of sins, according to the riches of his grace...*

(Ephesians 1:5-7)

In Ephesians 4:24 and 5:9 Paul uses righteousness to refer to being upright in character and conduct: *"**Put off your old self**, which is **being corrupted** by its deceitful desires; to be made new in the attitudes of your minds; and **to put on the new self**, created to be like God in true righteousness and holiness"* (Ephesians 4:22-24 NIV).

Notice how the NIV is using the present-continuous-tense when it says, *"...is being corrupted."* Our fallen nature will only grow increasingly worse until we completely *"put off"* our old self. This is a direct responsibility, as is *"PUT ON the whole armour of God."*

In Isaiah 60:1 it instructs us to, *"Arise, shine; for thy light is come, and the glory of the LORD is risen upon thee."* It does not say, *"God will raise you up and shine for you."* No! WE must do it. In the same way we must *"put on the whole armour of God."*

"You can lead a horse to water, but you can't make it drink," is much the same as *"you can lead a person to knowledge, but you can't make them think!"* How true. God has done *everything* for us - but has left much for us yet to do. For instance we must *apply* His truth to our daily lives. We are accountable to stir ourselves to *act-upon* and *live-out* all of our responsibilities - in Christ.

Salvation is *"free"* but this must not be interpreted by our flesh to mean: *cheap-with-zero-effort-or-responsibility-necessary!* Of course this is not the case. Instead the bible is loaded with instructions that require our willingness and obedience.

Daily Pursuit & Application

Only willing application can reap the fruits of scriptural prerequisites. **Pursuit** *(not discretion)* **is our heavenly obligation when it comes to TRUTH.** Have you ever noticed that faith is not necessarily polite and does not need to be in order to function? This is why raw faith is so often misinterpreted as arrogance! How David's older siblings viewed him, just before he slaughtered Goliath!

Daily application of and obedience to the truth is necessary in order to produce substantial change in our lives, *(see Romans 12:2 and Isaiah 1:19)*. Behaving, thinking and acting like people whose lives are truly, *"hidden with Christ in God"* (Colossians 3:2-3 NIV).

Therefore righteousness then is as a condition of the heart that is *actively* determined to follow the right path in life. In other words, how can we tell that someone is really a Christian? They behave like one. *(If you walk like a duck, and sound like a duck, then you must be a duck!)*

> So *if you're serious about living this new resurrection life with Christ, <u>act like it</u>. Pursue the things over which Christ presides.* Don't shuffle along, eyes to the ground, absorbed with the things right in front of you. Look up, and be alert to what is going on around Christ - that's where the action is. See things from his perspective. Your old life is dead. Your new life, which is your real life - even though invisible to spectators – is with Christ in God. **He is your life.**
>
> (Colossians 3:1-3 MSG)

❖

CHAPTER 4

Footwear of Readiness

Sharing the *"gospel of peace"* does not always generate or trigger *peace*; on the contrary it often stirs up much strife and conflict. Still it is called the *"gospel of peace"* that produces inner peace for all those *"…who believe."*

*With your **feet fitted** with the **readiness** that **comes** from the gospel of peace.*

(Ephesians 6:15 NIV)

*I am not ashamed of the **gospel of Christ:** for it is the power of God unto salvation **to every one that believeth;** to the Jew first, and also to the Greek.*

(Romans 1:16)

All peace comes at a hefty price. Customarily persecution has been aroused whenever and wherever the gospel has been preached, which seems to contradict the *"peace"* element of the *"gospel of peace."* Including the fact that Jesus told us, *"I did not come to bring peace but a sword."*

We Must Not Preach a False Gospel

The truth of the matter is that Jesus did not come to bring a *false peace.* Instead He brought true peace and the false always *conflicts* with the genuine.

They have seduced my people, saying, Peace; and there was no peace...

(Ezekiel 13:10)

The challenge that lies at the door of each and every disciple is not to succumb to the temptation of preaching a **false gospel** that declares false peace and a false sense of security. We are not commissioned to please everybody nor be politically correct all the time. *(The gospel has never been popular!)*

The fact is that they've lied to my people. They've said, "No problem; everything's just fine," when things are not at all fine. *When people build a wall, they're right behind them slapping on whitewash. Tell those who are slapping on the whitewash, "When a torrent of rain comes and the hailstones crash down and the*

*hurricane sweeps in the wall collapses, **what's the good of the whitewash that you slapped on so liberally, making it look so good?"***
(Ezekiel 13:10-12 MSG)

Only the true gospel can produce true peace and readiness, which affects each and every piece of our armour - inside and out! The Commission we received *(our purpose - to preach the gospel of peace)* encompasses, embraces and influences everything else.

The gospel of peace is the message of salvation *(peace* <u>*with*</u> *God)*. We are commissioned to go throughout the earth telling all people that they can have eternal peace <u>with</u> God through Christ. That peace has been restored between them *(mankind)* and God through Christ's redemptive work on the cross. Anyone, anywhere - can now have peace with God as a result.

*Ye are all the children of God by faith in Christ Jesus. For as many of you as have been baptized into Christ have put on Christ. **There is neither Jew nor Greek, there is neither bond or free, there is neither male nor female: for ye are all one in Christ Jesus.***
(Galatians 3:26-28)

*So, friends, we can now - without hesitation - walk right up to God, into "the Holy Place." **Jesus has cleared the way by the blood** of his sacrifice, acting as our priest before God. **The "curtain" (veil) into God's presence is his body.***
(Hebrews 10:19-21 MSG)

A Two-Fold Peace

HOWEVER it's possible to have peace WITH God without walking in the peace OF God. Yet to be effective soldiers *(ready in season and out to share this good message of peace with God)* we must not only have peace with God ourselves, but also operate continuously in the peace OF God - for others.

- Peace **WITH** God *(salvation/repentance)*.
- Peace **OF** God *(obedience/relationship/lifestyle)*.

We can know peace WITH God at the very moment of salvation, but the peace OF God *(needed for service and lifestyle)* must be stoked daily.

The prerequisite to having peace *WITH* God is *continuing* in the peace *OF* God. Our lifestyles must never become *detached* from His ruling, governing, and inner peace.

> *The kingdom of God is not meat and drink; but righteousness, and **PEACE**, and joy in the Holy Ghost.*
> *(Romans 14:17)*

Menacing Foot-Wear

Consequently, identifying the Roman soldier's footwear, as *"shoes-of-peace"* is a common misconception, especially considering how gruesome they were designed to be and how scripture clearly denotes them as *"shoes of readiness"* NOT *of peace.*

Perhaps better understood as "carriers" of peace, because of our charge to distribute the gospel of peace *(without delay or preference)*. In order to transport this gospel to the entire world, we as soldiers encounter spiritually hostile territory and must wade through and tackle some rough spiritual terrain.

All soldiers must be organized and ready in a moment's notice - to mobilize into position - ready to do business *(even at the risk of losing their lives)*. Their high-tech-equipment able to deal with any climate they encounter; with stealth, accuracy and speed. Therefore we too must be ready to transport this gospel, through thick and thin, *(without a moments delay)*, being confident, ready and equipped - to follow the Holy Spirit's lead.

The Ministry of Reconciliation

Preparing the way for people to accept *peace-with-God* is called the ministry of reconciliation. However this involves *much* spiritual warfare. The devil doesn't take it lying down when we enter his territory to win souls for Christ! So peace comes from the gospel, but certainly not from our shoes. Our shoes technically make way for peace.

War is a means to an end. In other words, the purpose of warfare is peace - not the fight. Each country must defend its borders and issue watchmen on the walls day and night to defend its inhabitants. Again - the purpose of war is *not* war. *(War for the sake of war is tyranny)*. The purpose of war is to enforce victory and peace. Every nation's history has been forged by countless wars, which are always very costly *(many lives are spent)*.

All war is for keeps! Meaning that whatever is won through battle, is for keeps and spiritual warfare is no exception. The devil fights for keeps. It is our duty as soldiers of the cross, to enforce the victory that Christ secured *"...triumphing over them by the cross"* (Colossians 2:15 NIV).

*[God] disarmed the principalities and powers that were ranged against us and made a bold display and public example (exhibition) of them, in **triumphing over them** in Him and in it [the cross].*

(Colossians 2:15 AMP)

Ready, Equipped & Duty-Bound

A soldier's position of readiness is two-fold:

- **Offensive:**
  Mobilized and ready to preach.
  (Proactive in transporting the gospel of peace)

- **Defensive:**
  Mobilized and ready for battle.
  (To defend and confirm the gospel)

Both postures are obligatory. A soldier who gives his/her life - to military service - **is duty-bound to be ready at ALL times and to follow orders!**

*Preach the word; **be instant in season, out of season;** reprove, rebuke, exhort with all longsuffering and doctrine.*

(2 Timothy 4:2)

I can't impress this on you too strongly... **proclaim the Message with intensity;** *keep on your watch. Challenge, warn, and urge your people.* **Don't ever quit.**
(2 Timothy 4:1-2 MSG)

As for the Roman soldier's shoes let's take a closer look at the FACTS, which help create an accurate picture of what Paul was referring to in Ephesians 6:15.

Designed for ACTION Not for Peace!

Firstly the Roman soldier's shoes were no ordinary shoes, they were more like boots that were made up of two parts: the shoe and the greave *(which completely covered and protected the lower leg and the foot)* and was finished off with 3-inch *(7.62cm)* spikes. *Not so peaceful!*

Such leg-wear or "boots" were certainly not passive but designed for ACTION - for serious business - both offensively and defensively.

- **The Shoe:**
  The Roman soldier's shoe was comprised of a mixture of durable leather and metal, with the sides held together with multiple pieces of robust leather. However on the bottom were affixed exceedingly menacing nails, some even three inches *(7.62cm)* long! Planned not only for holding the soldier firmly in his place, but also designed for kicking, maiming and even slaying his adversary. *(Once again this is clearly NOT a very peaceful piece of equipment!)*

- **The Greave:**
  The greave was the part of the Roman soldier's shoe that made it much more like a boot than a shoe! It was made of ornamental metal from the top of the knee to rest upon the upper portion of the foot. This was a vital piece of equipment for the soldier, who would have faced certain death with an injured leg or foot. **An immobile soldier - is a dead soldier!**

Just one skilful kick from his opponent and the bones of a soldier could easily shatter, if not adequately protected. So the greave was an essential piece of this warrior's garb, which ensured maximum protection and kept the solider critically *mobile* throughout battle.

Notably, the greave not only offered the Roman soldier protection *(for the lower leg)* from battle injuries but also gave effective protection during long marches, when he must walk through hazardous terrains.

Note: A brief side note that I want to insert here refers to an old military practise concerning the chopping off of big toes and thumbs! We see this in Judges 1:6 where king Adoni-bezek had his cut off - but not before he had done the same to no less than seventy other kings before him. Whom he had forced to grovel at his table, in humiliation: *"Seventy kings with their thumbs and big toes cut off had to gather their food under my table. As I have done, so God has repaid me."*

With no thumbs or big toes a solider would no longer have any grip or balance. With impaired equilibrium and such deliberate handicap - He would for the rest of his life be an incapacitated warrior *(no longer capable to grip the sword or bow and arrow that he was trained for, but neither farm equipment nor any other meaningful form of sustaining himself).* Obviously it would have been far less cruel to have killed these men, than to humiliate them for the rest of their lives.

No soldier wanted to be incapacitated. Even after military life, he would require basic skills for living. Such injuries would affect his entire future. Needless to say that the soldier's armour was vital - *not least his shoes!*

The Spikes of a Running Shoe!

Returning to the Roman soldier's specially designed footwear, *SPEED* was also very essential. By way of a short example, my wife Jenny was once a competitive athlete in her youth; with some of her teammates progressing to compete professionally, at such events like the British Commonwealth Games and the Olympics.

Her running gear was expensive - not least her shoes. She had a special bag, called her "spike bag," which kept the shoes, along with tools for cleaning, tightening and changing her spikes *(according to weather and terrain; either for cross country or for track),* so that she could compete to the best of her ability.

Incidentally on her initiation day at the athletics club, while being shown around the stadium, she recalled someone with a booming voice, suddenly crying *"TRACK!"* Followed by a thunderous troop of men who ran past her nearly knocking her off her feet! Such was her first lesson in track-safety and how to avoid being mowed down by a bunch of burly guys - with spikes in their shoes!

Spikes were used in all weathers - longer spikes for cross-country events *(particularly if the rain had made it muddy)* and shorter more stumpy spikes for sprinting, to grip the dry pink asphalt and in particular giving plenty of *thrust* for the starting line.

Grip and stable footing give advantage to both runners and soldiers. The only disadvantage is being trampled! *(As my wife found out - runners don't intend to stop - so it's always the pedestrian's responsibility to get out of the way!)*

In conclusion, the Roman soldier's powerfully protective footwear *(essentially legwear)* adequately symbolises *(spiritually)* the importance of staying ready, alert and prepared to *mobilise* at all times, to share this *"gospel of peace."* Which consequently involves **knowing how!**

1 Peter 3:15 instructs: *"... give an answer to every man that asketh you a reason of the hope that is in you."*

Through thick and thin, **keep your hearts at attention,** *in adoration before Christ, your Master.* **Be ready to speak up and tell anyone who asks why you're living the way you are** *and always with the utmost courtesy.*
(1 Peter 3:15 MSG)

Part of knowing *"how"* involves allowing the Holy Spirit to put the right words in our mouths, at the right time - no matter what the surrounding circumstances! We must be sensitive to His lead, *"... the Holy Spirit will make his witness in and through you"* (Mark 13:11 MSG).

When they shall lead you, and deliver you up, **take no thought beforehand what ye shall speak, neither do ye premeditate: but whatsoever shall be given you in that hour, that speak ye: for it is not ye that speak, but the Holy Ghost.**

(Mark 13:11)

CHAPTER 5

Carriers of Peace

So peace influences our whole equipment not just our feet. Our ability to stay in a position of readiness is influenced by peace and just as *"character"* is essential for the soldier - **peace is also crucial for the soldier's *inner life* and his ability to stay focused.**

As an overlapping influence, peace doesn't just help us remain ready in season and out but equally influences our thought lives *(helmet)* and our hearts *(breastplate)*. The gospel of peace involves much more than just our shoes!

> *God's peace [shall be yours, that tranquil state of a soul assured of its salvation through Christ, and so fearing nothing from God and being content with its earthly lot of whatever sort that is, that **peace], which transcends all understanding shall <u>garrison and mount guard over your hearts and</u> <u>minds</u> in Christ Jesus.***
>
> (Philippians 4:7 AMP)

> *Thou wilt keep him in **perfect peace, whose mind is stayed on thee:** because he trusteth in thee. Trust ye in the Lord forever: for in the Lord Jehovah is everlasting strength.*
>
> (Isaiah 26:3-4)

Peace then is vital in making us effective and successful in our overall mission *"It's wonderful what happens when Christ displaces worry at the centre of your life"* (Philippians 4:7 MSG).

Calm & Sober Composure is Vital

Fretful soldiers don't make effective soldiers. Composure is important. Otherwise rather than being Spirit led, a soldier would be misled by his own emotions and instincts. Nervous energy and being *"troubled"* about everything, is not the correct aptitude for a soldier.

A soldier who is too keenly anchored to his own flesh *(emotions)* is more than likely to react *(in error)* rather than respond *(correctly)* to the leading of the Holy Spirit: *"He has given us a spirit of power and of love and of* **calm and well-balanced mind** *and discipline and self-control"* (2 Timothy 1:7 AMP).

Soldiers who become trigger happy or go AWOL are similar to those who become overly judgmental and critical and begin to turn-in on one another:

> **If you bite and devour one another...** *be careful that* **you... are not consumed by one another...** *walk and live [habitually] in the [Holy] Spirit* **[responsive to and controlled and guided by the Spirit];** *then you will certainly not gratify the cravings and desires of the flesh (of human nature without God).*
>
> (Galatians 5:15-16 AMP)

Plus 1 Peter 5:8 says to us:

> **Be well balanced (temperate, <u>sober</u> of mind),** *be vigilant and cautious <u>at all times</u>; for that enemy of yours, the devil, roams around like a lion roaring [in fierce hunger], seeking someone to seize upon and devour.*
>
> (AMP)

We Cannot be Easily Overwhelmed

We must be like the eye of a storm - although surrounded by chaos - our core must be calm, well balanced and at peace. A perfect example of this would be the day that Jesus defused the storm on the lake. They set out because He said, *"Let us go over unto the other side of the lake"* (Luke 8:22-25).

We know that this particular trip did not turn out to be a particularly peaceful outing! Instead, *"…there came down a storm of wind on the lake; and they were filled with water, and **were in jeopardy**."* Instinctively these hardened fishermen *(some of them)* estimated that they were going to sink. *(Familiar with boats and all kinds of weather conditions, these men could usually handle a storm!)* However this particular storm had them completely freaked out.

So when scripture states that they *"were in jeopardy,"* their danger and vulnerability was valid. Yet where was Jesus in all of this commotion? Verse 23 reveals that, *"as they sailed he fell asleep…"* Looking at His heavy work schedule, it's not hard to see why He needed some rest.

Never Taken Off-Guard

In countless circumstances Jesus revealed that He was *full* of peace and composure, regardless of location. So once He had given the instruction to *"go over to the other side,"* Jesus had no reason to doubt His crew of capable men and took His opportunity for some well-earned R&R. Rest-bite from the demanding crowds - a power-nap! Whatever it was, Jesus had probably prayed all through the previous night and ministered through the following day - so His natural body would have demanded a break - as would ours!

After His rude awakening, Jesus was not taken off guard and did not once join the panic-party His disciples were having! Instead He remained calm and collected. He took charge of the situation with ease. How nice to imagine taking everything in our stride like this! Yet only the supernatural peace of God can produce such consistent behaviour in our lives, where nothing fazes, alarms or catches us off guard. **Every soldier needs this kind of peace; he can't afford to be so easily overwhelmed.**

Jesus did not Bring Religious Harmony

There exists an individual peace and a corporate peace, but the challenge for either is to **remain** in that state of peace *(insulated by God's peace)*, especially when there is *zero* peace in our outward circumstances or surroundings.

The gospel clearly brings conflict outwardly but is meant to bring peace inwardly. In Matthew 10:34 Jesus said: ***"Do not suppose that I have come to bring <u>peace</u> to the earth. I did not come to bring <u>peace</u>, but a sword...*** *a man's enemies will be the members of his own household."*

According to the Greek language *(Strong's #01515 "eirene")* this <u>peace</u> has everything to do with prosperity, unity, completion and quiet rest! **However Jesus did not bring religious harmony!**

He knew that even families would be disrupted and torn apart by such religious disharmony: *"I have come to turn a man against his father, a daughter against her mother, a daughter-in-law against her mother-in-law..."* (Matthew 10:35 NIV)

The Message Bible uses more contemporary terms, ***"Don't think I've come to make life cosy."*** Jesus did not come to make everybody *best-friends* or *one-big-happy-family*. No! He knew that His truth would seriously *"offend"* and cause great division and separation. In other words, Jesus was savvy to the fact that preaching unadulterated truth would cause revival in reverse! *"Do you too desire to leave me?"* (John 6:67 AMP)

> *Blessed (happy, fortunate, and to be envied) is he who* **takes no offense at Me** *and finds no cause for stumbling in or through Me and* **is not hindered from seeing the Truth.**
>
> (Matthew 11:6 AMP)

Up-Close & Personal

As we continue looking at the Roman soldier's outfit it's good to remember that Paul had first-hand experience of Roman soldiers. He was arrested on numerous occasions and spent much time in the presence of Roman soldiers - for prolonged periods of time *(depending on the period of his detention)*.

This meant that Paul became very accustomed with the Roman soldier's armour; he got to see each piece of equipment up-close! All of which aided his accurate attention to detail, when God gave him revelation about the *"full armour of God"* in the sixth chapter of the book of Ephesians.

Notice however that in 1 Thessalonians 5:5 Paul only had a partial revelation of the armour - we know this because he only gave an incomplete picture of the suit of armour saying: *"...be sober, putting on the breastplate of faith and love; and for an helmet, the hope of salvation."* (Remember that the New Testament is not in chronological order).

No shoes were mentioned for example, yet by the time of the writing of Ephesians, Paul had a complete revelation of the *"full* armour of God," which included the soldier's shoes of preparation!

Preparing the Way for a King

At this point I want to highlight some more, the meanings of *"readiness and preparation,"* to ensure that we understand their biblical context. For instance our contemporary understanding of such words would be: *eagerness, willingness, enthusiasm or keenness* - all of which describe an *attitude of readiness.*

However to measure up with their original meanings in scripture we can turn to the King James Version, which uses the word *"preparation"* instead of readiness, *"...your feet shod with the **preparation** of the gospel of peace"* (Ephesians 6:15).

The Greek language reveals to us that this particular word has a much weightier connotation than mere *eagerness,* which is overly simplistic. Preparation in the Greek language for instance, incorporates *everything* to do with *"making ready."* More specifically *"making necessary preparations."*

It is very proactive and drawn from the oriental custom of *"sending on, before kings - who were on their journeys - persons to level the roads and make them passable."* Therefore the context that is drawn into scripture here by the Greek language is this: **"... to prepare the minds of men to give the Messiah a fit reception and secure His blessings!"** *(See Strong's #2091 "hetoimasía" het-oy-mas-ee'-ah /#2090 "hetoimázō" het-oy-mad'-zo)*

John the Baptist

This brings to mind the role of John the Baptist: *"The voice of one crying in the wilderness, **Prepare ye the way of the Lord, <u>make his paths straight</u>"** (Matthew 3:3). Including the time when Jesus rode into Jerusalem and the people used their own clothes and palm branches to line His path! *"They cheered: Hosanna! Blessed is he who comes in God's name! Yes! **The King of Israel!"** (John 12:13 MSG)

> *They brought the donkey and the colt and laid their coats upon them, and He seated Himself on them [the clothing]. And **most of the crowd kept spreading their garments on the road, and others kept cutting branches from the trees and scattering them on the road.***
> *(Matthew 21:7-8 AMP)*

If we are not cultured or aware of historic events, then much of what we read in scripture *(relating to the time that it was written in)* will remain an enigma to our contemporary minds. Yet these people knew they were treating Jesus like a king; they had an early understanding of the significance of what they were doing. Their behaviour was relevant to how they would have treated a king in their own era *(as the Strong's definition revealed above)*.

They even lined his "ride" *(donkey)* with their clothes! Not much of a gesture for a dignitary such as a king perhaps, yet in those days such performances were very significant and Jesus knew it. It was recognition of His status *(albeit politically charged and motivated)*.

In addition this event showcased the fickleness of humanity; undoubtedly the same people crying *"Hosanna"* were the same crowd shouting, *"crucify him,"* not many days later! Nevertheless Jesus indulged the people, *(allowed them to treat Him like a king),* only so prophecy could be fulfilled. It was *NOT* an ego trip! Jesus also knew His popularity was going to be very short-lived!

> *Rejoice greatly, O Daughter of Zion! Shout aloud, O Daughter of Jerusalem!* **Behold, your King comes to you;** *He is [uncompromisingly] just and having salvation* **[triumphant and victorious], patient, meek, lowly, and <u>riding on a donkey</u>,** *upon a colt, the foal of a donkey.*
> (Zechariah 9:9 NIV)

In any case, this all aids our minds in grasping this whole context of *"preparation"* and *"readiness" (as relating to the shoes of a Roman solider).* And from such we know that we can never cease to share this gospel of peace, which prepares the way for our King *(Jesus the living Word of God).*

So our shoes are all about preparation in both tenses - present and future: making smooth His path here and now *(preparing people's hearts and minds to receive Him)* but also accommodating His soon coming and tangible return journey. That's why the gospel must never cease to be shared on this earth, until that final moment!

Our job as soldiers is to possess the ground and smooth out the path: *"Every place that the sole of your foot shall tread upon, that shall I give unto you…"* (Joshua 1:3)

Using Every Available Platform

This involves entering the public domain and preaching the truth from every available platform, as well as creating new ones! Preaching the gospel over the airwaves helps prepare the atmosphere *(using modern technology such as cyber space and the Internet)* so that individuals can be prepared to receive Christ and the message of salvation.

> *For the same Lord over all is rich unto all that call upon him. For* **whosoever shall call upon the name of the Lord shall be saved.**
>
> *How then shall they call on him in whom they have not believed? And* **how shall they believe in him of whom they have not heard?** *And* **how shall they hear without a preacher?** *And how shall they preach, except they be sent?*
>
> *As it is written,* **How beautiful are the feet of them that preach the <u>gospel of peace</u>,** *and bring glad tidings of good things!*
>
> (Romans 10:12-15)

Notice incidentally, how it is called the *"gospel of peace"* and not the *"gospel of truth."* This is because each individual in the entire world still has the opportunity, through Christ, to make **peace with God**.

Divine Purpose & Commission

Jesus, undeterred, went right ahead and gave his charge: **"God authorized and commanded me to commission you: Go out and train everyone you meet, far and** *near, in this way of life, marking them by baptism in the threefold name: Father, Son, and Holy Spirit. Then instruct them in the practice of all I have commanded you. I'll be with you as you do this, day after day after day, right up to the end of the age."*

(Matthew 28:18-20 MSG)

We can only share the gospel if we *know* it, which involves *diligence* and application on our part, *"…He is a rewarder of them that <u>diligently</u> seek Him"* (Hebrews 11:6). We cannot herald or propagate a message we are not familiar with or haven't any revelation of! All **true disciples** have been commissioned to preach this living gospel.

Making disciples NOT converts - is our mission - to the *entire* world as Christ's own ambassadors. Preaching reconciliation (2 Corinthians 5:20), and to be witnesses in the power of the Holy Spirit (Acts 12:8).

As with the rest of the armour, our shoes enable us to stand with firm footed confidence - as we share this gospel of peace. We should never be caught without our boots on. Ready to march, through thick and thin, to get this Gospel to the world - **both to defend and confirm its message.**

Seeing Jesus in Us

Often people do not care what we say, until we convince them we care. Our life-styles must preach more than we do! In other words, **if people don't recognise that we have been with Jesus, something is seriously lacking.**

Now when they saw the boldness of Peter and John, and perceived that they were unlearned and ignorant men, **they marvelled; and they took knowledge of them,** **that they had been with Jesus.**

(Acts 4:13)

Never Underestimate Peace

Although the gospel of peace does not always bring harmony, we are recognised by the presence of His peace in us, as we share His gospel. **We must never underestimate the power of peace in our lives.**

When I ask congregations, *"Do you have peace in your personal lives right now?"* mostly their reaction is to turn very quiet on me - they instantly go very thoughtful! The reason: they simply can't lie, not with their spouse *(or children)* sitting right next to them in the congregation, who know the reality of home life - behind closed doors!

We must be carriers of peace - otherwise we undermine our own position within the Kingdom. *"The Kingdom of God is... peace... in the Holy Ghost"* (Romans 14:17).

Strife Reveals an Absence of Peace

Strife is a killer. *"Where... strife is, there is confusion and every evil work"* (James 3:16). Strife is an absence of peace and too many times we allow strife and daily stresses to rob our peace - of mind and heart.

Once we learn to guard peace, peace will guard us!

God's peace... which transcends all understanding, *shall garrison and mount guard* over your *hearts and minds* in Christ Jesus.

(Philippians 4:7 AMP)

❖

CHAPTER 6

Formidable Shield of Faith

The Roman soldier had more than one shield, *(once again this was for public ceremony and military parades)*. What we can take from this is that each piece of the soldier's weaponry had its cosmetic imitation *(counterfeit of the real thing)* that was totally unsuitable for battle.

Once again, Ecclesiastes says there is a time for everything, so there's even room for ceremony, but we must never be duped or fall foul of using the wrong type, on the wrong occasion!

Our flesh loves to look good; it's all about *"appearances" (favouring cosmetics and all things shallow),* because life is just one big parade!

> **Lift up over all** the [covering] shield of saving faith, upon which you can quench **ALL** the flaming missiles of the wicked [one].
>
> (Ephesians 6:16 AMP)

The authentic fighting tool that we are focusing on here was one of two shields that the Roman soldier possessed. Unlike its counterpart the full sized version was actually able to save his life!

It usually measured four and a half feet high by two and a half feet wide *(ca. 140cm x 76cm),* and was oval in shape. It consisted of two layers of wood glued together and was covered with numerous layers of leather *(animal hide).* It was large enough for the soldier to squat behind and be *completely* shielded.

The Tortoise Formation

The Greek word *theron (door)* was used to describe this particular shield, because it was shaped long and wide like a door and could completely *"cover"* the Roman soldier. In addition to this *(during sieges and approaching walls)* the soldiers would lock shields to create the **"testudo formation"** *(Latin for tortoise).* This was particularly effective in ensuring fewer casualties and acted much like a tank would today.

What an awesome illustration of how effective *"unity"* can be for the Body of Christ and how working together can create fewer casualties, especially in spiritual warfare.

> Behold, **how good and how pleasant it is for brethren to dwell together in unity...** *for there the Lord has commanded the blessing...*
>
> *(Psalm 133:1,3 AMP)*

In his book "Dressed to Kill" Rick Renner writes the following:

"In the majority of cases, the Roman soldier's shield was composed of multiple layers of thick leather that were firmly laid on top of a foundation of wood. Usually six layers of animal hide were specially tanned and then **woven together so tightly that the shield became nearly as strong as steel.** One layer of leather is tough, but six layers of tightly woven leather made the Roman soldier's shield extremely durable, exceptionally strong, and nearly impenetrable.

Although these six layers of animal hide made the soldier's shield strong and durable, the shield could become stiff and breakable over a period of time if he didn't take care of it properly. Therefore the Roman soldier had to know how to maintain his shield in top-notch condition. **Every morning one of his first tasks was to attend to his shield - applying oil and then rubbing it deep into the leather to keep it soft, supple, and durable in the middle of a fight.** Failing to properly maintain one's shield was an invitation for a fatal blow.

Without a fresh touch of the Holy Spirit's power on your life, your faith will become hard, stiff, and brittle. If you ignore your faith and allow it to go undeveloped, never seeking a fresh anointing of God's Spirit to come upon your life, your faith won't be soft, supple, and pliable enough to stand up under attack when a challenge comes your way. Faith that is ignored nearly always breaks and falls to pieces during a confrontation with the enemy.

Flaming arrows would be dipped in pitch, lit, and fired at the Roman soldier but frequently before battles, the soldiers would place their shields in water *(leaving them there until they were completely saturated)* so to extinguish the flaming arrows, which would bury themselves into their shields. These shields would cover the soldiers from head to foot extinguishing the arrows and resisting the enemy. It is the same for us; the Shield of Faith will completely protect us and will resist the attacks of the enemy.

> *Your enemy the devil prowls around like a roaring lion looking for someone to devour.* ***Resist him, standing firm in the faith.***
>
> *(1 Peter 5:8b-9a)*

In order for us to keep our shield of faith in top-notch condition, we must give serious attention to the condition of our faith. We must make certain that we are allowing the Holy Spirit to freshly anoint our lives on a daily basis as we regularly saturate our faith with the water of the Word. **Word-saturated faith will always extinguish the devil's attacks!"** *[Renner, p350-352]*

Early Stealth Technology

Three types of arrows were used by the military during New Testament times. Regular arrows, similar to those still used today in competition *(with a bow)* and secondly ones dipped in tar and set ablaze before being shot into the air. Finally the last type, were arrows of *stealth*.

They were narrow but hollow and could be filled with combustible liquids that would ignite on impact! They were stealth because they were not easily detectable, silent as they passed through the air, not ablaze in flight, therefore invisible in the sky, without leaving a trail. They were often mistakenly identified as harmless, until they burst into flames on impact!

Evidently stealth technology has always existed, not just in modern warfare. But in today's world stealth technology has advanced and refers mainly to *"avoiding detection."* Whether interfering with radar, or reducing visibility in infrared, audio or radio frequency, you-name-it the military have thought of it!

Furthermore even though Satan deems himself an *artist* at *"absconding,"* **NOTHING slips the radar with God in the equation; everything becomes** *detectable*. As believers we have nothing to fear - we are on the winning side!

*Fear them not therefore: for **there is nothing covered, that shall not be revealed;** and hid, that shall not be known.*

(Matthew 10:26)

When Paul was writing about *"fiery darts"* in Ephesians 6:16 it is unmistakable that this particular type of arrow was what he had in mind. It carried fire and exploded once contact with its target had been accomplished.

Hostile Distractions

Such a picture of stealth and menacing arrows - adequately depict the relentless attacks we endure against our minds. Our thought lives are bombarded with combustible arrows night and day - seeking to set our emotions ablaze and out of control.

It often takes little for our minds to spin out of control. Just a minor suggestion about past events, or even recent hurts and we do the rest; spiral into a fit of anger. Just one arrow can set our entire day on fire!

However - according to the military - the best defence is offence and from a Christian point of view the best option that we have is to fix our eyes firmly on Jesus:

Looking away [from all that will distract] to Jesus, *Who is the Leader and the Source of our faith [giving the first incentive for our belief] and is also its Finisher [bringing it to maturity and perfection].*
(Hebrews 12:2 AMP)

When we go on the offensive, in order to obey the commission that Christ gave us, Satan does not take this challenge lying down. No! He fights back - using strategic flaming arrows. In Isaiah 54:17 it assures us that, *"No weapon that is formed against us shall prosper."* However this particular word *"formed"* reveals something specific about our enemy - that he is eager to *"fashion" (tailor-make)* assaults to flawlessly fit our situation.

The Evil Genius has been Overcome

Watching humanity for generations has allowed him such *"genius"* status, as seen here in John 16:11 from the Amplified version of the bible: *"The ruler (evil genius, prince) of this world [Satan]."*

A genius - because he knows just how to *manipulate* human nature! He is familiar with all the right triggers that best suit our personal profiles. He knows our individual *"specs" (specifications)* and will use such *intelligence* to stir up as much misery for us as possible, *(not content with just issuing headaches!)*

Nothing short of a *major strategist* - Satan is not willing to make many mistakes, preferring instead to take all the time necessary for his plans to take shape and have the maximum effect in our lives.

> *But I fear, lest by any means, as the serpent* **beguiled Eve through his subtlety (cunning),** *so your minds should be corrupted from the simplicity that is in Christ.*
> *(2 Corinthians 11:3)*

Faith Reveals itself in Action

Satan attacks everything connected with our lives: our churches, organizations, spouses and children, businesses. Everything he can influence - he will. Our only shield against such attacks is faith. Nevertheless our **faith must be active to be effective:** *"faith by itself, if not accompanied by action, is dead"* (James 2:17).

Nothing *"dead"* can protect us. So it's imperative to keep our faith in tip-top condition, like the Roman soldier's shield, it must remain supple and not brittle.

We must believe in God's ability to protect us and have confidence in His Word, ***"Satan is judged and condemned and sentence already is passed upon him"*** (John 16:11 AMP).

Hebrews 11:1 says, *"Now faith is being sure of what we hope for and certain of what we do not see."* Faith that is the substance of things hoped for is always *now* faith. If faith is not now, it is not faith. If it is not faith that is ***present tense,*** it is not the substance of things hoped for. Hope is always out there in the future.

It is easy to miss the implication and application of faith; very often we confess hope but think that we are confessing faith. It's quite simple: **hope sees but faith acts.** In addition God has done all that He is ever going to do about such things as: salvation, healing, finance, Satan and much more. Instead what we need to know is what God has already DONE and act upon that. This alone is our basis for faith.

God's Will is Expressed in His Word

God has already spoken and made promises to His children about their circumstances. His Word is His Will. Faith is an active moving force, which moves Christians forward. Jesus said to His disciples that if they had faith in

God and did not doubt in their hearts whatever they said would come to pass. This same truth applies to us.

> *Have faith in God... I tell you the truth, if anyone says to this mountain, "Go throw yourself into the sea," and **does not doubt in his heart but believes that what he says will happen, it will be done for him.** Therefore I tell you, whatever you ask for in prayer, believe that you have received it, and it will be yours. And when you stand praying, if you hold anything against anyone, forgive him, so that your Father in heaven may forgive you your sins.*
> *(Mark 11:23-25)*

CHAPTER 7

The Helmet of Salvation

The kind of helmet used in the first century and commonly used in the Roman army during Paul's time, was a beautiful piece of equipment that was highly decorative and yet one of the most important defences that the Roman soldier had.

It was elaborately ornate and intricate, with exquisite etchings, engravings and designs, sporting a huge plume of feathers (or coloured horsehair) that stood vertically from the top of the helmet. In public parades and ceremonial moments, this had quite the visual impact!

Usually made from bronze it not only protected the top of the head but also the ears, cheeks and jaws *(often with a hinged visor for added protection)* - little could penetrate a helmet like this! Furthermore, in an effort to make it more comfortable *(due to it's sheer weight)* the interior was typically lined with sponge.

Firmly in Place

TAKE *the helmet of salvation.*

(Ephesians 6:17)

The Greek compound word for helmet is: *perikephalaia (peri means: around/kephalaia means: head)* - which portrays: *something protective tightly fixed around the head.* Tightly fixed - because the soldier could not afford to misplace his helmet in the heat of battle. So it wasn't just resting on top of his head like a decoration!

It was fixed firm and not without good reason. Battle-axes were common in the day of the Roman soldier and were designed to take a soldier's head clean off his shoulders! So without this type of helmet *"tightly fixed"* in place on his head, the Roman soldier was asking for some serious trouble.

So the helmet of the Roman soldier was designed to be striking and notable, but was also a totally effective life preserver that was utterly vital to his survival.

Protecting our Thought Lives

Now the word *"survival"* is not a word I like much. Simply because too many of us procrastinate when it comes to spiritual warfare and as a result, spend most of our time *"surviving"* rather than *"thriving."* As the scripture reveals below, we are meant to reign in this life!

> ***How much more will those who receive God's abundant provision** of grace and of the gift of righteousness **reign in life** through the one man, Jesus Christ.*
>
> (Romans 5:17 NIV)

Many believers today lack protective headwear, for their minds and equivalent thought lives. They step out without their helmets firmly fixed in place and wonder why they nearly get their heads knocked off! With splitting headaches, severe stress and the mounting difficulty to concentrate, they become incapacitated to protect their own though lives.

Unrelenting bombardments against our minds occur every single day - not helped by a host of technologies, social media platforms and entertainment outlets - that are all loaded and laced with both disturbing and potentially harmful content.

Flammable Thoughts

Fiery darts with a cocktail of flammable and combustible thoughts such as: fear, hatred, suspicion, depression and mistrust; along with all manner of other interferences, target our minds relentlessly.

Torment by nature is designed to be *"relentless."* As seen here in 1 John 4:18, *"...because fear hath torment."* In the English language torment is synonymous with affliction: plagues, distresses, sufferings, annoyances and every kind of irritant. However in the Greek it refers more towards punishment and penalty.

On a daily basis we face considerable levels of filth to filter *(if we are disciplined)*. However for the undisciplined mind, the long-term effects of such oppression on our minds will unquestionably generate some serious consequences, such as: ill health, mental disorders, and many other kinds of *afflictions*.

Let me interject here, that when a woman is pregnant, she becomes vitally aware of her diet. Not wanting to harm the baby's growth in any way she considers more what she puts in her mouth. She knows that there is a consequence to everything she puts in her mouth during those months, especially if she does not want to gain unwanted weight!

We must be as rigorous with our minds as the pregnant woman is with her weight and her diet! I have witnessed my wife during such periods in her life. She becomes very conscientious and puts in extra effort.

Where our minds are concerned, what we feed - we breed. *Anything* that goes in there, without being filtered, will have "consequences" and we cannot afford, in any way to be lax with our minds because a disciplined *(not legalistic)* mind, is a sober mind. Exercising "restraint" is part of our lives. Whenever "any-thing-goes" in society - bondage is fast approaching!

The Renewed vs. The Fallen Mind

The bible instructs us to *renew* our minds - because the condition of our minds is a key element to change *(transformation)* in our lives. Where our minds go *(wander)* our lives inevitably follow. The governments of this world are beginning to wake up to this fact. Today mental health is a real concern the whole world over, simply because it's affecting growing numbers of the work force, which in turn affects the economy and then warrants some weighty attention!

In a BBC News Article that appeared online in October 2012, Labour leader Mr. Ed Milaband, spoke about "vast changes" that were needed across society to tackle mental illness. The article was entitled: "**Mental illness - biggest UK health challenge.**"

> *The problem of mental illness in the UK is the "biggest unaddressed health challenge of our age... it blights the lives of millions, costing UK business £26bn and the NHS an extra £10bn a year... Meanwhile, the annual costs to UK business are £15bn in **reduced productivity**, £8.5bn in sickness absence, and £2.5bn to **replace staff who can no longer work.**"*

Britain is not alone; governments across the world are being forced to address similar issues in their own countries; society breaking down due to mental illness.

This might appear to be a side issue and what does it have to do with spiritual warfare? Everything! The helmet of salvation protects our minds - *if applied*. However, those without Christ have no protection at all and such is the fruit and consequence of living without the mind of Christ or the helmet of salvation.

> *Do not conform any longer to the pattern of this world,*
> *but **be transformed by the renewing of your mind**.*
> *Then you will be able to test and approve what God's will*
> *is - his good, pleasing and perfect will.*
>
> (Romans 12:2 NIV)

To *"renew"* refers to: *refurbishing and renovation!* The Greek word *(Strong's #342/341) anakaínōsis* means: *"complete change for the better; to make new… to be changed into a new kind of life as opposed to the former corrupt state."*

All of the above is strictly unachievable without Jesus Christ - the living Word of God. Only the Word of God has the power to cleanse our minds, *"…by the washing of the water of the Word"* (Ephesians 5:26).

The application of such truth demands that we *completely* change our way of thinking. This is like saying: as much as we would never enter battle without our helmets; equally we should never enter battle with our old mind-sets. **Moreover, just as babies cannot be taken into battle, nor can the helmet of salvation cover the old mind-set *(fallen nature).***

Deliberately Leading Every Thought Captive

So it is imperative that we read and meditate on His Word and keep His commands and remain obedient to them. We must read, meditate and speak the Word continually, *"meditate on it day and night... careful to do everything written... Then you will be prosperous and successful"* (Joshua 1:8).

The following scripture is a vital reference to how we should be dealing with our minds.

> *For though we walk (live) in the flesh,* **we are not carrying on our warfare according to the flesh and using mere human weapons.** *For the weapons of our warfare are not physical [weapons of flesh and blood], but they are mighty before God for the overthrow and destruction of strongholds,* **[inasmuch as we] refute arguments and theories and reasonings and every proud and lofty thing that sets itself up against the [true] knowledge of God; and we lead every thought and purpose away captive into the obedience of Christ** *(the Messiah, the Anointed One)...*
>
> *(2 Corinthians 10:5 AMP)*

The above scripture is very *"on-subject"* for this particular chapter. Our minds are an integral part of spiritual warfare. As a for instance: Joyce Meyer's on-going top selling book for many years has been, *"The Battlefield of the Mind."* Her top selling teaching materials centre on three major topics: 1) The Mouth 2) The Mind 3) The Emotions. Revealing that Christians are struggling in specific areas *"on-mass"* and are seeking to overcome.

In the Message translation, this same passage reads:

The world is unprincipled. It's dog-eat-dog out there! **The world doesn't fight fair. But we don't live or fight** *our battles that way - never have and never will. The tools of our trade aren't for marketing or manipulation, but they are for demolishing that entire massively corrupt culture.*

We use our powerful God-tools for smashing warped philosophies, tearing down barriers erected against the truth of God, fitting every loose thought and emotion and impulse into the structure of life shaped by Christ. *Our tools are ready at hand for clearing the ground of every obstruction and building lives of obedience into maturity.*

(2 Corinthians 10:5 MSG)

The Power of Audible Meditation
(Chewing on the Word of God!)

Going back to Joshua 1:8 where it instructs us to *"meditate... day and night,"* we will look at what it means to meditate. According to the Vine's Complete Expository Dictionary *"meditate"* means: to *moan, growl, utter and to speak. (Notice: all are audible).*

This Hebrew word is common to both ancient and Modern Hebrew and is found only 25 times in the Old Testament. It seems to be an onomatopoetic term, reflecting the sighing and low sounds one may make while musing, at least as the ancients practiced it. Its first occurrence appears in Joshua 1:8, as above.

However perhaps the most famous reference to *meditating* on the law *"day and night"* is Psalm 1:2 where it says, *"... CHEW on Scripture day and night"* (MSG).

*His delight and desire are in the law of the Lord, and on His law (the precepts, the instructions, the teachings of God) he **habitually meditates (ponders and studies) by day and by night.***

(Psalm 1:2 AMP)

Clearly such *"meditation"* on God's Word, is the only answer to dealing with an un-renewed mind.

Now let's look at the Hebrew word for meditate in Psalm 1:2 above, which uses the word *"hagah"* that surprisingly expresses the *"growl"* of lions! (Isaiah 31:4) and the *"mourning"* of doves! (Isaiah 38:14). *[We could say that one is passive the other aggressive, yet both are audible].*

When the word is used in the sense of *"to mourn,"* it apparently emphasizes the sorrowful sounds of mourning, as seen in this parallelism: *"Therefore will I howl for Moab, and I will cry out for all Moab; mine heart shall mourn for the men of Kir-heres"* (Jeremiah 48:31).

The idea that mental exercise, planning, often is accompanied by low talking seems to be reflected by Proverbs 24:1-2: *"Be not thou envious against evil men, for their heart studieth destruction, and their lips talk of mischief."*

So *"meditation"* from the context of scripture is not a silent exercise *(or a new age ritual!)* rather it is very proactive. **Our private mediation of God's Word must involve the audible-aspect-of-study and should be applied day and night.**

Much like everything else about the armour of God - renewing the mind is both offensive and defensive. We can use the Word of God to defend our minds *(edify and build them up via spoken meditation)*. We can also use the Word of God in an offensive way, *(to declare: "it is written" in the same way Jesus did, when the enemy attacks)*.

However is this biblical discipline all too much trouble? Is it easier to meditate on what the world around us dishes up night and day instead - via the Internet, TV, radio and other sources? Let us make sure therefore, that ample time is given to the Word - not less time than we give to other things that have NO POWER to renew our mind-sets.

When we choose not to renew our minds, by applying ourselves, we'll always have more spiritual warfare than we bargained for - in fact it will be quadrupled! If we don't dip our entire lives in the water of God's Word and rub in the oil of the Spirit - we only make it harder for ourselves to overcome in life. **Only the *"renewed"* mind is a *"sound"* mind!**

If we don't see these spiritual implications to God's Word and the responsibility that is addressed to us, *(to be "doers" of His Word)*, then everything becomes mere mechanics; just dead letter and dead works, with no power to change.

Weaknesses of the Natural Mind

Notice the following weaknesses of the natural mind:

- It is hostile to God (Romans 8:5-7).
- Things of God are foolish to the natural mind (2 Corinthians 4:4).

- The natural mind is the source of violent and evil desires (Ephesians 2:3).
- It is futile in its thinking, darkened in understanding (Ephesians 4:17-18).

We have not received the spirit of the world but the Spirit who is from God, that we may understand what God has freely given us. This is what we speak, not in words taught us by human wisdom but in words taught by the Spirit, expressing spiritual truths in spiritual words.

The man without the Spirit does not accept the things that come from the Spirit of God, for they are foolishness to him, and he cannot understand them, because they are spiritually discerned.

(1 Corinthians 2:12-14 NIV)

Everything about our relationship with God is a partnership. We must do everything with Him and *nothing* alone. Anything we try to achieve in our own strength will fail and this includes the renewing of our minds. Daily application of truth is needed and who better than the Spirit of Truth to aid us in this vital quest?

Principles & Action to Obtaining a Renewed Mind

So we need the Holy Spirit before we can understand the things of God. So how do we go about renewing the mind?

Principles:

- We must completely surrender our minds to the Lord (Romans 12:1).

- We must submit our thinking to the Cross - Jesus (Ephesians 4:20).
- Make a deliberate choice about the place of our minds (Colossians 3:2).
- Read and meditate on the cleansing power of God's Word (Joshua 1:8).

Action:

- We must examine and test the content of our thought lives (Philippians 4:4-8).
- Immediately refuse every wrong thought (Philippians 4:6).
- Read and meditate on the Word (Joshua 1:8).

Some Signs of a Renewed Mind:

- Spiritual understanding increased (Ephesians 1:18).
- A change of life through understanding truth (Philippians 4:8-9).

The Mind becomes the Vehicle of the Holy Spirit

The mind becomes a tool and vehicle for the Holy Spirit *(i.e. gifts, discernment & revelation)*. However we must make a conscious effort every moment of every day to yield our minds to the Holy Spirit, until it becomes as natural as breathing! Always conscious of what we are thinking about, as scripture says: *"...take EVERY thought captive."* We can't afford to be casual or to procrastinate where our minds are concerned.

Self-control is a fruit of the Spirit, which the Holy Spirit brings into our lives. Part of a disciplined lifestyle is that we must stop living and speaking out of our emotions. Thinking out loud has gotten all of us into trouble! Whereas sharing in the right context can be helpful, but it must always be with the right people. However no one can have self-control *FOR* us. It has to be a conscious effort of our own.

The more we try to fix ourselves the worse we become and it's not "fixing" that matters so much as having more of Christ. As 1 Corinthians 2:16 says *"...but we have the mind of Christ."*

> *Who has known or understood the mind (the counsels and purposes) of the Lord so as to guide and instruct Him and give Him knowledge? But we have the mind of Christ (the Messiah) and do hold the thoughts (feelings and purposes) of His heart.*
>
> *(1 Corinthians 2:16 AMP)*

Someone who has the mind of Christ is someone who is continually operating in revelation knowledge. Revelation knowledge always brings about instant change, simply because it is received by the spirit, to transform the soul, and then has an outworking effect on the body. Although the change *begins* instantly, change can take a long time and is part of the sanctification process.

So the state of our minds then, influences everything we are and everything we do. It's vital that this part of our lives is surrendered to Christ and protected by the Helmet of Salvation.

To finish this particular chapter, I want to add some basic facts. It is well considered today that the human brain produces approximately 70,000 thoughts on an average day.

Plus if we include the thoughts that we process as we sleep *(note there are 86,400 seconds in a 24 hour day)* this then means that we have a different thought every 1.2 seconds!

I don't find this hard to believe. In fact I think that it's probably much more! Either way, this creates some hefty mental baggage, especially if we are ill equipped to deal with it.

Thankfully as believers we are well equipped, but there is such a thing as *"over-stimulation,"* that we can all fall foul of. It is something that concerns young children and babies, as well as adults. Some scientists today are linking *"over-stimulation"* to certain health conditions, due to the fact that our minds were never meant to process such a degree of activity *(without rest)* that they are subject to today.

Information overload, excessive amounts of entertainment, digital games and so on, can all be blamed for much of this. Our every day gadgets are both helpful and harmful simply because human nature never knows when to quit! We take computers to bed and wake up with them in the morning! We travel with them on the train, in the air and on the road. Quite simply there is access to the Internet *EVERYWHERE!*

From personal experience I know that my own mind is very active indeed and always has been. *(I am not alone!)* However I have learnt to be very disciplined with my mind over the years and this has helped me considerably. I simply *refuse* to be governed by my own natural mind *(will and emotions)* and choose instead to be governed by the mind of Christ.

❖

CHAPTER 8

The Sword
that the Spirit Wields

The Roman soldier did not use just one type of sword but had several. I will run through them briefly before we settle on the type that Paul had in mind when referring to the *"sword of the Spirit,"* in Ephesians 6:17.

TAKE the helmet of salvation and **the sword that the Spirit wields**, *which is the Word of God.*

(Ephesians 6:17 AMP)

- **The First Sword:**
  Known as the "Gladius," this sword brings to mind the word *"gladiator."* This was the first of five swords that the Roman soldier possessed, it was tremendously heavy and sported a very long blade. Although a handsome looking sword artistically, it was clumsy to use because of its sheer weight. It required two hands to use and was sharpened only on one side.

- **The Second Sword:**
  This sword was shorter and slimmer; roughly 17 inches *(43.18cm)* long and 2 ½ inches wide *(6.35cm),* which made it lighter and much easier to use.

- **The Third Sword:**
  This was a dagger-like sword - carried in a small sheath out of sight. In up-close combat it could be driven straight into his opponent's vital organs, especially the heart.

- **The Fourth Sword:**
  This particular type of sword was so protracted and slight *(primarily used by the cavalry, not the infantry)* it ended up being used more in competitive sports *(such as modern-day fencing)* and was not taken seriously in battle!

- **The Fifth Sword:**
  This *"máchaira"* sword is what we have all been waiting for! The one that Paul was referring to in chapter 6 of Ephesians; *"the <u>sword</u> (máchaira) of the Spirit."*

This particular sword was a merciless weapon, roughly 19 inches *(48.26cm)* long; it was sharpened on both sides of the blade and could cut in any direction. It was razor-sharp and usually had a curved tip, which made it particularly gruesome. In fact it was the most frightful of all the other swords because it could inflict a wound far greater.

By reason of its specially adapted curved tip and its two-edged blade, *(coupled with the Roman soldier's skilful handling),* when it was thrust and twisted inside an opponent's stomach, it caused his "entrails" to spill out on *withdrawal!*

So let's get this straight! Paul purposely likened the *"sword of the Spirit" (not to the lighter-sports-edition or the dagger-like-model, but)* to the most deadly and punishing sword available to the Roman solider at that time - how remarkable!

One thing is for certain, there was nothing passive about the Roman soldier and there should be nothing passive about us. He was trained and skilled. Why then do we fall into the things of God and expect to become experts over night? Practice makes perfect and we must learn to yield to the Holy Spirit - **Who has all the skill that we need!**

Just like the fruits of the Spirit *(not "seeds" of the Spirit!)* that come fully formed and ripe into our lives. The Holy Spirit does not need to be *"developed!"* Again, **WE are the ones who must develop and learn how to yield.** *(Even Jesus had to go through the process of "...learning obedience"* Hebrews 5:8).

Skilfully Handling the Rhema

Evidently the sword *"…that the Spirit wields"* (Ephesians 6:17b AMP), which is the **Rhema Word of God**, is something awesome and to be feared. Demons don't fear it for nothing. They see this weapon and fear it exceedingly!

However naturally speaking, perhaps an opponent might not fear a soldier's loinbelt to the same degree that he might fear his sword, but we are not speaking naturally! We have talked about the significance of the loinbelt already and how it must work together with all other aspects of the armour, none more so than the sword.

Now spiritually speaking we must see the significance between the Logos and the Rhema. Both are as necessary as the other and we must learn how to handle both, as we see in 2 Timothy 2:15 where it talks about *"…**rightly handling** and **skilfully teaching** the Word of Truth."* And in 1 Corinthians 3:10 where Paul the apostle says of himself, *"According to the grace… like a **skilful architect** and master **(expert) builder** I laid [the] foundation…"* (AMP/NIV)

I must point out again; that the Rhema Word of God is literally the sword *"… **that the SPIRIT wields**"* or more precisely, *"the sword **OF** the Spirit,"* which means that the *"máchaira"* is exclusively HIS! Plus He already knows - *better than any* - how to use *("wield")* this weapon with great proficiency! Therefore it stands to reason, that we don't just require knowledge of the written Word *(Logos)* but also knowledge of how to skilfully work with the Holy Spirit *(in partnership)* to use the Rhema accurately, as God planned.

It was the Holy Spirit after all who led Christ into the wilderness, and used revelation knowledge *(Rhema),* to defeat Satan in that particular battle. The same is true for us today; He will lead us into the right battles, at the right time, and then lead us out again, victorious! He will put the right words in our mouths at the right time: ***"For it will not be you speaking, but the Spirit of your Father speaking through you…"*** (Matthew 10:20 NIV)

We must have confidence in this Holy Spirit, who is not just sensitive like a dove but also powerful and intimidating, like a mighty rushing wind!

Rhema & Logos - Inseparable

Nevertheless, much like the rest of the armour, the loinbelt and the sword are inseparable. Rick Renner who brought out in his book, *"This weapon, called the 'sword of the Spirit,' has the potential to rip our foe to shreds"* also rightly pointed out that the two must *always* work together:

Just as the shield rested on a clip on the right side of the loinbelt, the sword hung from a clip on the left side of the loinbelt. The loinbelt thus served as both a support for the shield and a resting place for the soldier's sword.

As seen before, the loinbelt is representative of the written Word of God, the Bible. **The written Word of God is the <u>primary source</u> for a Rhema from God"** *[Renner, p408].*

- **Of the Rhema he said:**

"When you faced a precarious situation… the Holy Spirit reached into that reservoir of scriptures you have stored up in your heart through study, prayer and meditation and quickened a verse to your mind that helped you in your time of need."

- **Of the Logos he said:**

"You might say that the written Word, the Bible, is like the **'gladius'** sword of the Roman soldier - a broad-shouldered and extremely heavy blade. This huge blade is capable of making a sweeping blow against the enemy. On occasion, however, we need a specific **Rhema Word - a smaller, two-edged sword - to deal the enemy a fatal blow!"** *[Renner, p409-410]*

Clearly then, even though the *"máchaira" (Rhema)* in the right hands is terrifying to behold, not everyone who tries - poses a real threat! Meaning that demons know who's skilled and who isn't. Just look at the sheer indifference and irreverence that the evil spirit showed towards the seven sons of Sceva - who tried to copy Paul's authentic ministry!

> **God did unusual and extraordinary miracles by the hands of Paul...** *diseases left them and the evil spirits came out of them.*
>
> *Then some of the traveling Jewish exorcists (men who adjure evil spirits) also undertook to call the name of the Lord Jesus over those who had evil spirits, saying,* **I solemnly implore and charge you by the Jesus Whom Paul preaches!**
>
> *Seven sons of a certain Jewish chief priest named Sceva were doing this.* **But [one] evil spirit retorted, "Jesus**

I <u>know</u>, and Paul I <u>know about</u>, but who are you?"
(Acts 19:11-15 AMP)

The result? They ended up running from that house, violently *"stripped naked and wounded"* (verse 16).

Alive & Full of Power

For the Word that God <u>speaks</u> is alive and full of power [making it active, operative, energizing, and effective]; it is sharper than any two-edged sword, penetrating to the dividing line of the breath of life (soul) and [the immortal] spirit, and of joints and marrow [of the deepest parts of our nature], exposing and sifting and analysing and judging the very thoughts and purposes of the heart.

And not a creature exists that is concealed from His sight, but all things are open and exposed naked and defenceless to the eyes of Him with Whom we have to do.
(Hebrews 4:12-13 AMP)

- **The Rhema Word:** *(defensive)*

A Rhema Word is a word that is *spoken*, by the power of the Holy Spirit - to assist us in defending ourselves against the enemy.

- **The Rhema Word:** *(offensive)*

We are also told to proclaim the very manifold wisdom of God to the rulers and authorities in the heavenly realms:

*[The purpose is] that **through the church** the complicated, many-sided wisdom of God in all its infinite variety and*

*innumerable aspects might now **be made known to the angelic rulers and authorities (principalities and powers)** in the heavenly sphere.*

(Ephesians 3:10 AMP)

As we start to speak out God's Word, only then can light shine and dispel darkness, bringing freedom and liberty. Satan will very often bring temptation in many different forms, even trying to deceive us with the Word of God itself. This means that **we need to have an accurate understanding of scripture and to be able to discern when God is actually speaking to us.**

Feelings Don't Rule

In 1 Corinthians 2:15 it states that, *"The spiritual man makes judgements about all things."* Jesus of course knew the Word, as He was the Word and was able to discern truth, which is the Word of God, **rather than to allow His feelings to rule His decisions.**

- **Believe on His Word:**

*I tell you the truth, if anyone says to this mountain, "Go, throw yourself into the sea," and does not doubt in his heart but believes that what he says will happen, it will be done for him. Therefore I tell you, **whatever you ask for in prayer, believe that you have received it, and it will be yours.***

(Mark 11:23-24)

The above scripture is telling us to believe and not doubt, but goes on to say in verse 25:

And when you stand praying, if you hold anything against anyone, forgive him, so that your Father in heaven may forgive you your sins.

(Mark 11:25 NIV)

We must have no unforgiveness in our hearts but must come before Him with pure hearts (Psalm 66:18), with nothing against anyone:

- Confess our sin (1 John 1:9).
- Forgive as an act of our will (Matthew 6:14).
- Believe that we have received our forgiveness (Matthew 6:14).

To Defend & Oppose Truth at the Same Time is an Oxymoron!

As with the other pieces of armour, there are prerequisites to using the sword of the Spirit. Again it is HIS sword, not ours. Therefore obedience to His Word is the all-important criterion. Without which we disqualify ourselves. **We cannot work together with the Holy Spirit if we are opposed to His Truth!** *"Can two walk together, except they be agreed?"* (Amos 3:3)

We must *actively* agree with the truth - to be able to fight with it. **We cannot fight truth and defend it at the same time.** Likewise we cannot yield and resist at the same time. It's an oxymoron!

Rather as soldiers we must make a clear-cut decision to obey the Holy Spirit and **relinquish governorship of our**

lives over to Him. Otherwise the only battle we will ever face is that constant battle with ourselves, which never ceases and **renders us scathingly ineffective for the Kingdom of God.**

> *So that the righteous and just requirement of the Law might be fully met in us who live and move not in the ways of the flesh but in the ways of the Spirit [**our lives governed** **not by the standards and according to the dictates of the flesh, but controlled by the Holy Spirit**]...*

> *...those who are according to the Spirit and are controlled by the desires of the Spirit **set their minds on and seek those things, which gratify the [Holy] Spirit**...*

> *...**you are living the life of the Spirit, if the [Holy] Spirit of God [really] dwells within you [directs and controls you]**...*

> ***All who are led by the Spirit of God are sons of God...** you have received the Spirit of adoption [the Spirit producing sonship] in [the bliss of] which we cry, Abba (Father)! Father!*
>
> (Romans 8:4-15 AMP)

CHAPTER 9

Our Far Reaching Prayer Lance

When Paul talked about the "full armour of God" we know that he fashioned it upon the Roman soldiers armour. The "full" Roman armour of that time included the lance. Although not specifically mentioned - we can conclude that without mentioning it by name - Paul did include it when he included prayer. Without the lance the Roman soldiers outfit was not complete, likewise without prayer - nor is our armour complete. So in my opinion it is largely safe to assume that the lance refers to prayer and vice-versa - in keeping with the rest of the suit of armour that Ephesians 6 is fashioned upon.

> **Pray in the Spirit** *on all occasions with all kinds of prayers and requests. With this in mind,* **be alert and always keep on praying** *for all the saints.*
> *(Ephesians 6:18 NIV)*

The Roman soldiers used a variety of lances that ranged in size and shape, which of course like everything else evolved with use. Their design was altered and adapted over time to suit the needs of the Roman soldier.

Lances were made of wood with a metal tip - usually iron and could be up to seven feet *(ca. 2m)* in length - with a variety of different designs. However lances could come in different lengths, large and small, either for thrusting up-close or for launching through the air - at remarkable speeds and distances - especially in the hands of trained and experienced soldiers.

After taking down an opponent from a distance, a soldier could then follow-through with an up-close attack, to finish the job!

It was usually the more heavy "pilum" lance that would be flung at great distances to take out an enemy that was fast approaching but still far off - eliminating the threat - before they could gain ground. This was a typical plan of action when an encampment realized an oncoming attack.

Prayer is a Powerful Weapon

What a great picture for the heart of a prayer warrior! To comprehend how their prayers have such a far reaching effect and won't return void, *(so long as their prayers conform with scripture!)*

In Ephesians 6:18 Paul instructs believers: *"pray with all kinds of prayers,"* this includes praying in tongues. There is power in intercession, because at the same time, Jesus is interceding for us: ***"Christ Jesus... who is at the right hand of God and is also interceding for us"*** (Romans 8:34 NIV).

I like to ask the Lord when I pray, *"What is on Your heart Lord?"* What is Jesus praying? Because I want to be praying in line with His prayers - not the other way around! And the Holy Spirit will reveal the heart of God to us: *"The Spirit Himself [thus] testifies together with our own spirit..."* (Romans 8:16 AMP)

The Comforter (Counselor, Helper, Intercessor, Advocate, Strengthener, Standby), the Holy Spirit, Whom the Father will send in My name [in My place, to represent Me and act on My behalf], ***He will teach you all things****. And* ***He will cause you to recall (will remind you of, bring to your remembrance) everything I have told you.***
(John 14:26 AMP)

People typically like to say that God is in *"complete"* control. My comment to this would be both: *"Yes AND no!"* John Wesley once said: *"It seems that God is limited by our prayer life, that He can do nothing for humanity unless someone asks Him."*

We must understand the basics: Jesus reclaimed the authority that humanity had given away in the Garden of Eden. Despite this fact however, God chose prayer/intercession to be the instrument by which His power was to be released here on earth *(as it is in heaven)*. [This is why Jesus - the son of man/Son of God - is *STILL* praying! Romans 8:34]

So the power of God is at our disposal, waiting for us to call Him into action, so long as our lives are in conformity with His Word.

While Jesus restored dominion and control back to humanity as it was in Eden, this can only be enforced in conjunction with His Spirit *(partnership)* and His Word *(obedience)*. This means that in order to enjoy dominion here and now, we must work in partnership with God. Likewise for God to have control here on earth now - He must work in partnership with man *(He limited Himself to this arrangement!)*

God is looking for Men and Women who will Stand in the Gap

So who is willing? Who will intercede, who will spend time in an act of intercession? We talk about reaping a harvest, very often we want to be in there reaping, getting involved in the action, but we need to spend time standing in the gap as well. We can only be fruitful if prayer has been the main business of the day. Then at the time of ministry we will see the fruit.

In Joel 2:13 we are told to *"Rend your heart and not your garments."* We need to give birth. *"Yet no sooner is Zion in labour than she gives birth to her children"* (Isaiah 66:8). That is a very profound statement, taking Zion to represent the church, if we go into labour in intercession/into a state of childbirth, praying then becomes an active event.

Every mother will know that at the time of giving birth, it is a very active and not necessarily a pleasant experience. The mother does not necessarily care who hears her or even watches at the time. She is so taken up with the need to give birth. Intercession *(travailing in the Spirit)* is giving birth to the things of God and it is on most occasions a noisy activity.

Just like groans of travail precede the birth of a baby, so too is Holy Spirit intercession, i.e. ***travailing in the Spirit brings to birth new life, new hope, and new possibilities for those who are trapped in seemingly impossible situations.***

God promises in Joel that when you rend your heart, crying out in giving birth, that *"afterward, I will pour out my Spirit on all people"* (Joel 2:28). I know from watching my wife giving birth to each of our children that it was agony, as Jesus foretold. But a moment after the child is born and laid upon the mother's breast, the pain is forgotten and the joy of new birth overwhelms her.

When interceding/praying perhaps for another person, there will be times when you will know in your Spirit that the breakthrough has happened. You will know this breakthrough by the experience of joy. You can rejoice that your prayers have been received and answered in the Spirit realm. That is when you see results in the natural realm, but not before the breakthrough has been given.

Power in the Face of our Enemy

When the enemy shall come in like a flood, the Spirit
of the Lord shall lift up a standard against him and
put him to flight [for He will come like a rushing stream
which the breath of the Lord drives].

(Isaiah 59:19 AMP)

If you want to see the Spirit of God move more than
He has already, say on a housing estate, witnessing to the
unsaved. Then you must be willing to intercede and get into
an attitude of bringing God's will into being, travailing for
them. You will then reap the harvest that God has prepared.

My dear children, for whom I am again in the pains of
childbirth until Christ is formed in you.

(Galatians 4:19)

Paul was constantly in a place of weeping before God for
his people. This then should also be the place for us. Prayer
not only produces individual power, but it also produces
corporate power as well.

We must recognise that we have no power of our own.
But as we come before God in obedience, in submission
completely surrendered unto Him, i.e. dead to self, with
a servant's heart completely broken before Him, He will
release His power into our lives. We must depend on His
power, the power of the Holy Spirit and not depend on man-
made power.

Not by might nor by power, but by my Spirit, says the
Lord Almighty.

(Zechariah 4:6)

108

In ourselves we can do nothing, but in Christ we can do all things. Because it is He who gives us the strength by His Holy Spirit so that we can be successful in our prayer lives. God's Word must be foremost, because as we feed on His Word we are building His words into our inner self.

When coming to God in Prayer/Intercession we must:

- Pray, to the Father in the Name of Jesus (John 16:23).
- Pray, according to His will (1 John 5:14).
- Pray, without doubting (James 1:6-7).
- Pray, with a pure heart (Psalm 66:18).
- Pray, fervently *(loudly)* (Luke 18:7).
- Thank God for answered Prayer (Colossians 4:6).

More than Conquerors

*Yet amid all these things we are **more than conquerors** and gain a **surpassing victory through Him Who loved us.***

(Romans 8:37 AMP)

We must remember that Jesus has made us more than conquerors and that we have power in prayer because:

- He has set us free (Colossians 1:13).
- He was triumphant at the cross (Colossians 2:15).
- We can approach the Throne of God with confidence (Hebrews 4:1).
- Satan is under our feet (Luke 10:19).
- We have authority in Jesus' Name (Matthew 10:1).
- We have overcome him *(Satan)* by the blood of the Lamb (Revelation 12:11).

Never has Satan been a Threat to God!

At this point I want to add a quotation by Bill Johnston who looks at spiritual warfare from a different angle than most, teaching on this particular topic in the Body of Christ today. As I always reach for balance I want to quote Bill from his recent book: "Hosting the Presence" as he sights some justifiable concerns:

"Never at any time has Satan been a threat to God... (Who is uncreated - has always existed) whereas Satan is limited in every way. God gave him his gifts and abilities at his own creation. There has never been a battle between God and Satan. The entire realm of darkness could be forever wiped out with a word. But **God chose to defeat him through those made in His own likeness - those who would worship God by choice.** Brilliant! It was the issue of worship that brought about his rebellion in the first place.

Satan was never the focus... I become concerned by an overemphasis by some on the subject of spiritual warfare. Spiritual conflict is a reality that is not to be ignored. Paul admonishes us to not be unaware of the enemy's devices (see 2 Corinthians 2:11). We must be mindful of his tools. But even so, **my strength is putting on the full armour of Christ. Christ is my armour!**

...light drives away darkness without a fight. I can't afford to live in reaction to darkness. If I do, darkness has had a role in setting the agenda for my life... **Jesus lived in response to the Father. I must learn to do the same...**"

Called into a Place of Strength & Intimacy

"The devil doesn't mind negative attention. He'll let us chase him all day long in the name of 'warfare.' But it's a place of <u>weakness</u>. **God calls us into a place of strength - rediscovering our place in the Garden, walking with Him in the cool of the evening.**

It is from a place of intimacy that true warfare is experienced. Perhaps it was for that reason that David, Israel's greatest warrior and king, wrote, *'You prepare a table before me in the presence of my enemies'* (Psalm 23:5). The place of fellowship and intimacy with God is seen as the table of the Lord - yet it is placed in front of His enemies."

He goes on to say about the Israelites and the Promised Land:

"God had given the entire Promised Land to the children of Israel. **It all belonged to them all at once.** It was their inheritance by promise. But they possessed only what they had the ability to manage. **The expression of God's dominion flowed through them according to their ability to rule well.** God told them why He wouldn't give it to them all at once - the beasts would become too numerous for them (see Exodus 23:29; Deuteronomy 7:22). **They were to grow into possessing the fullness of their inheritance.**

The same principle applies to us today. From the Garden of Eden to Israel and the Promised Land to the believers of this hour, **it's all ours.** But what we possess now is according to our capacity to steward in the way that He would…

Now in the same way God had given Adam and Eve the <u>entire planet</u> to rule over, they only had possession of the Garden of Eden. **There is always a difference between what's in our account and what's in our possession...** They too were to grow into their inheritance. They owned it all by promise. But their control was equal to their maturity. They possessed only what they could steward well" *[Johnson, p34-37]*.

❖

CHAPTER 10

Exalting the Name &
The Blood

God has highly exalted Jesus above every name. And as the scripture below says, every knee shall bow and every tongue shall confess of those in heaven and on earth that Jesus Christ is Lord and that includes Satan and his demonic hosts. Our spiritual authority is based upon the *"blood of the Lamb;"* Christ's death and the shedding of His blood at Calvary destroyed Satan's claims and rights.

*Therefore God exalted him to the highest place and gave him **the name that is above <u>every</u> name**, that at the name of Jesus every knee shall bow, in heaven and on earth, and every tongue confess that **JESUS CHRIST is LORD**, to the glory of God the Father.*

(Philippians 2:9-11 NIV)

Satan is *already* defeated and we have the authority to speak directly at him and his demons in the Name of Jesus. Jesus Himself spoke directly to Satan, *"get behind me, Satan"* (Matthew 16:23), when Peter allowed himself to be an instrument of the devil. Jesus also at the time of His temptation in the wilderness spoke in authority directly to Satan (Matthew 4:1-11).

In verse 10 Jesus said to him: *"Away from me Satan, for it is written: 'Worship the Lord your God, and serve Him only.'"* Then the devil left Him (verse 11). And James also tells us to *"Resist the devil and he will flee from <u>you</u>"* (James 4:7). Satan will flee when <u>we</u> speak not in our own authority but in the authority, which Jesus has given us in the power of His Name. Jesus has given us authority over **ALL the power of the enemy.**

In the following scripture Jesus recalls seeing Satan falling from heaven:

He said to them, I saw Satan falling like a lightening [flash] from heaven.

*Behold! **I have given you authority and power** to trample upon serpents and scorpions, and [physical and mental strength and ability] **over ALL the power that*** *the enemy [possesses]; and nothing shall in any way harm you. **Nevertheless, do not rejoice at this, that the spirits are subject to you, but rejoice that your names are enrolled in heaven.***

(Luke 10:18-20 AMP)

I really like the following verse: *"In that same hour He (Jesus) rejoiced and gloried in the Holy Spirit..."* as He gave thanks to God. Awesome to see Jesus so happy! Another translation says: *"At that time Jesus, full of joy through the Holy Spirit..."* So what was Jesus so happy about? He understood the gravity of what He had just said! Something that we need to get ecstatic about too!

We have absolute assurance through Christ, yet Satan will always try and do all he can to frighten and prevent believers from using the weapons that God has given. He does not care what we say about him, he does not fear or flee from anyone - unless they speak in the authority that Jesus gave them. *The authority of the Name of Jesus comes with revelation of the victory that He won at Calvary.*

We don't *assume* authority - nor do we stumble across it. We accept it - humbly and grow in great confidence. For Jesus is LORD!

Our Visible Praise & Worship Pierces the Darkness!

Music is the most powerful force on the earth. Scientifically light travels at approximately 186,000 miles per second, travelling at such a high speed that it carries a threshold of audio-ability *(sound being music or song)*. The bible tells us: **"You are all sons of the light..."** (1 Thessalonians 5:5) God is light and in Him there is no darkness. Our worship unto Him is light.

> *Every good gift and every perfect gift is from above, and* **cometh down from the Father of lights,** *with whom is no variableness, neither shadow of turning.*
>
> *(James 1:17)*

What we see with our human visibility is about 3% of the light spectrum. Now if God were to readjust our human visibility from 3% to 40% of the light spectrum, we would actually be able to see our own worship *(worship being light)!* So as we worship God, our worship *(light)* attacks the darkness and principalities and powers of the air. This in turn dispels and drives them away.

Psalm 22:22 says: *"I will declare your name to my brothers; in the congregation I will praise you."* So every time we worship God, Jesus comes in our midst and begins to praise His Father. And as we worship the Lord, **God not only hears our praises but He <u>sees</u> them also.**

So as we are worshipping God, our worship *is* actually dispelling the kingdom of darkness. As sons and daughters of light, we are worshipping the Father of Light, and that worship **defeats Satan.**

> **You are all sons of the light** *and sons of the day; we do not belong either to the night or darkness.*
>
> *(1 Thessalonians 5:5 AMP)*

The Blood of our Sacrificial Lamb

*For Christ, our **Passover Lamb** has been sacrificed.*
(1 Corinthians 5:7b NIV)

To understand fully the implications of what happened at Calvary when Jesus died on the cross *(the Second Passover)* we need to look in Exodus 12:1-13, to the *First Passover.*

The Lord said to Moses and Aaron in Egypt,

*This month is to be for you the first month, the first month of your year. Tell the whole community of Israel that on the tenth day of this month each man is to **take a lamb for his family, one for each household**. If any household is too small for a whole lamb, they must share one with their nearest neighbour, having taken into account the number of people there are. You are to determine the amount of lamb needed in accordance with what each person will eat.*

*The animals you choose must be year-old males **without defect**, and you may take them from the sheep or the goats. Take care of them until the fourteenth day of the month, when all the people of the community of Israel must slaughter them at twilight.*

***Then they are to take some of the blood and put it on the sides and tops of the doorframes of the houses** where they eat the lambs. That same night they are to eat the meat roasted over the fire, along with bitter herbs and bread made without yeast. Do not eat the meat raw or cooked in water but roast it over the fire, head, legs and inner parts. Do not leave any of it till morning; if some is left till morning you must burn it.*

This is how you are to eat: with your cloak tucked into your belt, your sandals on your feet your staff in your hand. Eat it in haste; it is the Lord's Passover. On that same night I will pass through Egypt and strike down every first born - both men and animals - and I will bring judgement on all the gods of Egypt. I am the Lord. *The blood will be a sign for you on the houses where you are; and when I see the blood, I will pass-over you. No destructive plague will touch you when I strike Egypt.*

(Exodus 12:1-13 NIV)

Notice in the third verse it says *"tell the whole community of Israel that each man has to take a lamb for his family and his household."* The words **"whole community"** implies that God wants to reach all, for the scriptures tell us that Jesus was the reconciliation of the whole world (Romans 11:15), every single person, man, woman, and child.

This Passover was God's protection and provision for His people. The blood that was sprinkled upon the door-posts was for protection, a sign for deliverance not only from death, but also from the slavery of Egypt. One thing that we can be sure of as Christians is that we are in the world but not of it (2 Corinthians 10:3).

Set Free from Slavery

We have been set free from being enslaved to the world, through the overcoming Christ (Romans 12:2). The bitter herbs remind us of the suffering that we went through in the world.

As long as we stay under the protection of the blood, for we have been washed in His blood (Hebrews 9:14), we can remain free from sickness and disease that so often can afflict. For when Satan sees the blood of Christ, there is no way that he is able to inflict, for scripture says no destructive plague will touch you. Jesus stripped the enemy and having disarmed the powers and authorities, He made a public spectacle of them, triumphing over them by the Cross (Colossians 2:15).

When Christ came as High Priest of the good things that are already here, He went through the greater and more perfect tabernacle that is not man made. That is to say, not a part of this creation.

He did not enter by means of the blood of goats and calves. But He entered the most Holy Place once and for all by His own blood, having obtained eternal redemption.

The blood of goats and bulls and the ashes of a heifer sprinkled on those who are ceremonially unclean sanctified them so that they are outwardly clean. How much more, then, will the blood of Christ, who through the eternal Spirit offered himself unblemished to God, cleanse our consciences from acts that lead to death so that we may serve the living God!

(Hebrews 9:13-14)

The New Covenant

For this reason we know that Christ became the new covenant that we might receive an eternal inheritance. He was the only ransom, which could be given to set us free.

For when Christ came into the world, He said:

Sacrifice and offering you did not desire, but a body you prepared for me; with burnt offerings and sin offerings you were not pleased. Then I said, "here I am - it is written about me in the scroll - I have come to do your will - O God."

(Hebrews 10:5-7)

By one sacrifice He has made perfect forever those who are being made holy. The Holy Spirit also testifies to us about this. First He says:

This is the covenant I will make with them after that time, says the Lord, I will put my laws in their hearts, and I will write them on their minds.

(Hebrews 10:16)

The blood that Jesus shed for us cleanses us from every sin as long as we confess them to God and receive forgiveness (1 John 1:7-9). If we live under the protection of the blood of Jesus, Satan is unable to get a foothold within our lives (Ephesians 4:27). We as believers must know where we stand in God. The blood of Jesus enables us to live victoriously over Satan (Revelations 12:11).

The blood of Jesus, the shedding of His blood and His not failing once, in any of the smallest details, resulted in Satan's defeat; cancelling his claims upon the entire human race.

The Blood of the Lamb Defeated Satan

Through the blood of Jesus we are:

- Cleansed from sin and forgiven (1 John 1:9).
- Justified (1 Corinthians 6:11).
- Have access into His presence (Ephesians 2:18).
- Sanctified, and made holy (1 Corinthians 6:11).
- Have victory over Satan (1 Corinthians 15:57).
- Are redeemed (Ephesians 1:7).

CHAPTER 11

Equipped with Power

So often we forget as Christians that God is ready and willing to put into motion the heavenly host to war against the hosts of evil. There are many passages in scripture, which show that the un-fallen angels have a ministry of able "assistance" for the saints here on earth, which includes the involvement of spiritual warfare as we will see. *(The Message Bible uses the term, "God-of-Angel-Armies" see Psalm 46:11).*

*Are not the angels all **ministering spirits** (servants) sent out in the **service** [of God for the **assistance**] of those who are to inherit salvation?*
(Hebrews 1:14 AMP)

In Revelation 12 Michael and his angels are seen fighting against the dragon and his angels. The **united forces of the angelic hosts** and the Church are together in this battle and again we see the ministry of angels on behalf of the saints in Daniel 10 where Michael the Archangel resists the interference of the satanic prince of Persia.

Our Lord Jesus referred also to the legions of angels He could have called to His aid to protect and deliver Him during the hour of power and darkness.

*Do you suppose that I cannot appeal to My Father, and He will **immediately provide** Me with **more than** twelve legions [more than 80,000] **of angels?***
(Matthew 26:53 AMP)

However He chose to fight the battle through alone. Accepting no heavenly help. *(There were other occasions when Jesus was ministered to by angels, but it's important to recognise that they did not at any point "rescue" Him from His mission, rather "strengthened" Him. See also Matthew 4:11 and Luke 22:43).*

Likewise we know through scripture that God is also willing to send help, *(in the form of angels),* to help us in our hour of need. Look at Peter's miraculous escape from prison, even though soldiers *(under the orders of Herod)* were heavily guarding him.

So Peter was kept in prison, but the church was earnestly praying to God for him. The night before Herod intended to bring him to trial, **Peter was sleeping between two soldiers, bound with two chains, and sentries stood guard at the entrance. Suddenly an angel of the Lord appeared** *and a light shone in the cell. He struck Peter on the side and woke him up. "Quick get up!" he said, and the chains fell off Peter's wrists.*

Then the angel said to him, "Put on your clothes and sandals." *And Peter did so. "Wrap your cloak around you and follow me," the* **angel** *told him. Peter followed him out of the prison, but he had no idea that what the* **angel** *was doing was really happening; he thought he was seeing a vision. They passed the first and second guards and came to the Iron Gate leading to the city.* **It opened for them by itself.**

(Acts 12:1-17 NIV)

People in the Jerusalem church were gathered praying for Peter's release. Meanwhile (verse 13) Peter knocked at the outer entrance, the servant girl came and answered the door. When she recognised Peter's voice, she was so overjoyed she ran back without opening the door and exclaimed, *"Peter is at the door!"* (verse 14).

What did the church say? *"You are out of your mind"* (verse 15). That is so typical of us very often. We do not believe our own prayers; if God sent an angel would we really believe?

Our Assurance in Warfare:

- All is placed under our feet (Ephesians 1:21-23).

125

- He has given us His authority (Matthew 10:1).
- He *(Jesus)* that is in us is greater than he that is in the world (1 John 4:4).
- There is power in the blood of Jesus (Revelation 12:11).

Paul goes on to say, *"Be strong in the Lord."* That is we must rely on God's strength and not on our own.

Embark with Power

Jesus' power *(dunamis)* came through the empowering of the Holy Spirit. Notice Jesus did not embark upon His earthly ministry *without* the power of the Holy Spirit, which came upon Him during His baptism.

> *Now when all the people were baptized, and when Jesus also had been baptized, and [while He was still] praying, the [visible] heaven was opened and **the Holy Spirit descended upon Him in bodily form like a dove**, and a voice came from heaven, saying, You are My Son, My Beloved! In You I am well pleased and find delight!*
> *(Luke 3:21-22 AMP)*

Jesus was omnipotent *(having all power)* but He chose to lay this power aside until His time of baptism. He was God by His incarnation, when the Word became flesh and lived for a while among us, Jesus literally became a man.

> *The Word (Christ) became flesh (human, incarnate) and tabernacled (fixed His tent of flesh, lived awhile) among us; and we [actually] saw His glory (His honour,*

His majesty), such glory as an only begotten son receives from his father full of grace (favour, loving-kindness) and truth.

(John 1:14 AMP)

Hebrews 2:17 states that Jesus was made like his brothers. This means that He was 100% man through and through *(NOT half human and half divine as some would suggest).* However simultaneously Jesus always remained fully and essentially God (Colossians 2:9), yet laid aside some of the divine attributes of His glory, when He became a *man.*

He became a man so that He could fully communicate God's Word and God's love to us. He became a man to model our ministry in the world, and He became a man to represent our human nature on the cross.

Three Major Attributes of His Glory

The three main attributes of His divine glory, which He laid aside were:

- His Omnipresence - *everywhere-at-once.*
- His Omniscience - *all-knowing.*
- His Omnipotence - *all-powerful.*

Boldness is Not Docile or Fragile!

As long as we are hidden with Christ in God, we can afford to take a bold stand! But that's the key. Jesus is our victory. Without Christ there can be no victory. Militancy in Christianity refers to ACTION. We must have some *get-up-and-go* about us! We can't afford to be docile and fragile with a passive *(overly delicate)* spirit. Laziness and procrastination are *NOT* spirituality *(and an absence of luxury is "not" suffering!)*

It's too easy to procrastinate for years, refusing to fight saying, "Why should I? Why should I *have* to engage in this battle? However the quicker we realize that there is no choice, the better. Just looking back over our lives, we can quickly see how at every juncture there's been a battle attached *(even several!)* The real question is "do we want to thrive or survive? Because it's high time we develop some holy aggression, to protect what God has given us and stop expecting someone else to do it for us!

There are no two ways about it, we have been equipped for ACTION and only full-blooded drive, passion and determination will get this job done. Jesus displayed such energetic *"righteous indignation"* when He created a bit of a drama in the Temple:

> *Jesus went into the temple of God, and **cast out all them that sold and bought in the temple, and overthrew the tables of the moneychangers**, and the seats of them that sold doves... It is written, My house shall be called the house of prayer; but ye have made it a den of thieves.*
> (Matthew 21:12-13)

This was not a *mild-mannered-moment* for Jesus! He showed His feisty side and rightly so: *"Zeal for your house will consume me"* (John 2:17 NIV). Zeal represents intense passion and is something that passive people do not possess! They watch everyone else working hard and wonder what all the fuss is about! They criticise by saying, *"There's too much stress!"* But their lives are typically counterproductive. They have *nothing* to show for their faith and have forgotten that faith without *"works"* is dead. Even *"the working of miracles"* involves some *work!*

However just being productive for "self" doesn't count either! It's what we do for the Kingdom that counts - if we put God's house first the rest takes care of itself, *"Seek first the kingdom of God… and all these things will be added to you"* (Matthew 6:33).

God's message was delivered by the prophet Haggai to the governor of Judah, Zerubbabel… A message from God-of-the-Angel-Armies:

"The people procrastinate. *They say that this isn't the right time to rebuild my Temple… How is it that it's the 'right time' for you to live in your fine new homes while the Home, God's Temple, is in ruins?*

Take a good hard look at your life… you have spent a lot of money but you haven't much to show for it…

Do it just for me [rebuild the temple]. Honour me. **You've had great ambitions for yourselves, but nothing has come of it…** *While you've run around, caught up with taking care of your own houses, my Home is in ruins… because of your stinginess… I've matched your tight-fisted stinginess by decreeing a season of drought…* **nothing - not man or woman, not animal or crop - is going to thrive."**

(Haggai 1:1-11 MSG)

Putting God's house first is imperative. Obviously if we neglect to do the right thing, we can bring suffering upon ourselves. If you like, we can cause our own warfare and it's not the devil opposing us but our own actions. The consequences of which can be pricy.

If however, as genuine believers, we live in obedience to the best of our ability - without procrastinating - then we have every reason to be bold and spiritually forceful and vigorous. We are already aware that Satan won't ever take our progress lying down but will try and hinder us every inch of the way - nevertheless in Christ we are still *"more than conquerors..."* Satan's actions should not determine ours.

My bible says quite plainly:

*Indeed **ALL** who... are determined to live a devoted and godly life in Christ Jesus **will meet with persecution [will be made to suffer because of their religious stand].***

(2 Timothy 3:12 AMP)

Those who experience zero opposition *(or resistance)* are typically those who are doing zero for God! Equally those who are unproductive for God will always critically analyse those who are! There seems to be too many laid-back Christians, laid-back Christians don't need armour, but a cushion!

It's Time for all Believers to Wake Up!

Believers it's time to wake up!

*You know what [a critical] hour this is, **how it is high time now for you to wake up out of your sleep (rouse to reality).** For salvation (final deliverance) is nearer to us now than when we first believed (adhered to, trusted in, and relied on Christ, the Messiah).*
(Romans 13:11 AMP)

Listen to how this same scripture about spiritual slumber reads in the Message Bible:

Make sure that you don't get so absorbed and exhausted in taking care of all your day-by-day obligations that you lose track of the time and doze off, oblivious to God. *The night is about over, dawn is about to break.* **Be up and awake to what God is doing!** *God is putting the finishing touches on the salvation work he began when we first believed.*

We can't afford to waste a minute... *in sleeping around and dissipation, in bickering and grabbing everything in sight.* **Get out of bed and get dressed! Don't loiter and linger,** *waiting until the very last minute.* **Dress yourselves in Christ, and be up and about!**
(Romans 13:11-14 MSG)

Romans 11:8 calls this the, **"spirit of slumber [attitude of stupor]."** Just like the five virgins who, *"while the bridegroom tarried, they all <u>slumbered</u> and slept"* (Matthew 25:5).

It's no longer a time to be docile and drowsy; only fighting when we feel the need to defend ourselves. **This is NOT real spiritual warfare - it's just *self-preservation!* "The**

131

wicked flee when no man pursueth: but the righteous are bold as a lion" (Proverbs 28:1). Again the Message Bible reads slightly differently:

> *The wicked are <u>edgy with guilt, ready to run off even when no one's after them;</u> Honest people are relaxed and confident, BOLD AS LIONS.*
>
> *(Proverbs 28:1 MSG)*

We can't afford to be fixated on being defensive all the time, instead as we are dressed in the full armour of God, we must be ready to go on the offensive - just as every soldier is trained to do. When we are only defensive, then our spiritual warfare is sterile *(produces nothing!)* David's brothers sat listening to Goliath day after day, until their little-brave-heart of a brother *(the rooky)* came along and challenged the challenger! **David was ready for ACTION, when Saul and his entire army were in a state of** *terrified inertia!*

NOW is the time to *STAND* and to resist the devil and all his onslaughts *(that ceaselessly try to bring all sorts of corruption into the church)*. To *STAND* our ground, firmly in place, having done all that is required *(including face our responsibilities!)*

> *Put on God's complete armour, that you may be **able to resist and stand your ground** on the evil day [of danger], and, having done all [the crisis demands], **to stand [firmly in your place]**.*
>
> *(Ephesians 6:13 AMP)*

We do not always have to pray on our knees. We can employ all kinds of methods, volumes, and postures - just

132

so long as we pray in conformity with God's Word and in partnership with His Spirit. Like young David - we have confidence and can behave boldly because we have faith in God's Word.

Although lions are bold, they only roar loudly when necessary. They don't roar 24/7 nor do they need to! They are already convinced of their authority, the rest of the time they conserve energy! We too have a battle cry - when we need it - that carries great authority.

In Hebrews 11:30 is says, *"By faith the walls of Jericho fell down, after they were compassed about for seven days."* Notice it did not mention anything about shouting! Shouting had its place on the last day, but for seven days they were silent!

Insubordination Relinquishes Authority

A very important point that I want to emphasise here is that our strength is not dependant on our *"shout"* **but on our obedience,** *(we rule as well as we have been ruled!)* Notice in James 4:7 it says, ***"Submit yourselves therefore to God. Resist the devil, and he will flee from you."*** It's a simple equation: We submit. We resist. The devil flees from us. But what comes first - resisting the devil or submitting to God? Submission to God - of course - without which we have no hope of *"resisting the devil"* or seeing him *"flee!"*

God told Saul:

To obey is better than sacrifice and to listen than the fat of rams. For rebellion is as the sin of witchcraft, and stubbornness is as iniquity and idolatry.

Because thou hast rejected the word of the Lord, he hath also rejected thee from being king.

(1 Samuel 15:22-23)

Without submission we simply have no position of authority. In other words: **ZERO SUBMISSION EQUALS ZERO AUTHORITY.** And Satan, who is a legalist, knows whether we are *"submitted to God"* or not. **He also knows that rebellion cannot engage in spiritual warfare.**

We can't resist the devil if we have *any* common ground with him at all. Jesus explained this point, when some accused Him of casting out demons by *"Beelzebub!"*

Any kingdom divided against itself will be ruined and a house divide against itself will fall. *If Satan is divided against himself, how can his kingdom stand? I say this because you claim that I drive out demons by Beelzebub.*

Now if I drive out demons by Beelzebub, by whom do your followers drive them out? So then, they will be your judges. But if I drive out demons by the finger of God, then the kingdom of God has come to you.

(Luke 11:17-19)

Jesus demonstrated complete confidence, because He was in complete compliance *(submission)* **to the will of His Father at all times,** *"I have kept my Father's commandments"* (John 15:10). We have no power of resistance without submission and this particular revelation knowledge is vital when it comes to spiritual warfare. *"So be subject to God. Resist the devil* **[stand firm against him]**, *and he will flee from you"* (AMP).

Consider this, if the Israelites had not obeyed that day, and had spoken when they were instructed to be silent, would those walls still have fallen? I believe this type and shadow from the Old Testament was set up as a very poignant reminder for us: **NOT emphasising the power of silence nor our vocal chords but on our faithful submission!**

This is always the emphasis, which gives us our position of power. We must emphasise - not on fighting devils - but on our submission to God. However SUBMISSION alone is not enough. Jesus RESISTED the devil in the wilderness and so must we. That's why it says, "SUBMIT to God. RESIST the devil and he will flee from you." Otherwise it would simply have said, *"Submit to God and everything will be okay."* Or *"Submit to God and the devil will automatically flee from you!"* No! Even *with* submission - there is still a devil to *"resist"* but not BEFORE we submit to God.

Both "instruction" and "application" - are part of every soldier's career - he is vigorously trained to obey orders and follow instructions. It certainly does not pay to do otherwise:

> *The Lord said to me...* **Do not go up or fight, for <u>I am not among you</u> - lest you be dangerously hurt by your enemies...** *You would not hear but rebelled against the commandment of the Lord and were presumptuous and went up...*
>
> *(Deuteronomy 1:41-42 AMP)*

We cannot go into battle without the Lord. Without Him we have no confidence - just presumption *(relying on our own estimations, guesswork and arrogance)*. David said, **"Keep back** *they servant also from <u>presumptuous sins</u>; let them not have dominion over me: then shall I be upright, and I shall be innocent from the great transgression"* (Psalm 19:13).

Jesus alone is our victory:

The sting of death is sin, and the power of sin is the law. But thanks be to God! **He gives us the victory through our Lord Jesus Christ.**

(1 Corinthians 15:56-57)

Who shall separate us from the love of Christ? Shall trouble or hardship or persecution or famine or nakedness or danger or sword? As it is written: "For your sake we face death all day long; we are considered as sheep to be slaughtered." **No, in all these things we are more than conquerors through him who loved us.**

(Romans 8:35-37)

Because of Jesus we can operate in the same Holy boldness as He did: *"Now Lord... enable your servants to speak your word with great boldness"* (Acts 4:29).

New Testament Christians were not weak and wimpy; they were strong and enduring. Persecutions would not hinder their vision in any way. John the Baptist came boldly proclaiming to King Herod and the Chief Priests: *"Repent! For the Kingdom of God is at hand."*

His words were not filled with wimpy religious phrases. His message was clear, bold, blasting and to the point. He gave the Word of God boldly. The message in New Testament times was the same to all, to the powerful, the weak, the rich, the poor, the famous and the unknown, and it must be the same today. It should not matter what town or what church we are in, or part off, the message is the same.

Boldness needs to come back into the church and fear of retaliation must leave. We need God pleasers and not man pleasers, men and women who will boldly preach the Word of the Lord without compromise or losing position. We need boldness to proclaim that our faith in God works.

Fearless Confidence

*Because of my chains, most of the brothers in the Lord have been encouraged to **speak the Word of God more courageously and fearlessly.***

(Philippians 1:14)

We must be confident towards: Heaven and Earth.

- **Heaven:**
*In whom we have **boldness and access with confidence** through faith in Him.*

(Ephesians 3:12 NKJV)

We can come boldly before the throne of grace because of the blood of Jesus; we have access to the Throne of Heaven having boldness to enter the Holiest, by the blood of Jesus (Hebrews 10:19).

*Let us therefore **come boldly to the throne of grace,** that we may obtain mercy and find grace to help in time of need.*

(Hebrews 4:16 NKJV)

- **Earth:**

And for me, that utterance may be given to me, that I may **open my mouth boldly** *to make known the mystery of the gospel.*

(Ephesians 6:19 NKJV)

We are to be bold here on earth to boldly proclaim the Gospel of Jesus Christ to the people of the world. We must boldly use the name of Jesus, proclaiming the truth and that Jesus has the power and authority to meet every need. However when the Gospel of Jesus Christ is preached boldly, religious people in particular get disturbed and upset!

We as believers need to know who we are in Christ, to know that we have boldness and confidence in Him and that we do not have to fear the devil or any of his works because we have victory in Jesus' name, *"... be of good cheer; I have overcome the world"* (John 16:33).

In Christ we have Overcome

We must also stop looking at our weaknesses and shortcomings and begin to realize that we are the *"righteousness of God in Christ"* (2 Corinthians 5:21). So therefore we have a right to use the name of Jesus boldly against the devil. We can be bold towards Satan, his demons, sickness, disease, poverty and every evil work of the enemy, because of who we are in Christ, and say boldly to Satan "Satan you have absolutely no authority over me, because you are a defeated foe" (Matthew 18:18; Philippians 2:9-11; Colossians 2:15).

Demonic powers rule when Godly people are passive. They rule men and women of God who are not willing to stand boldly without compromise and to confront powers of darkness by praying and preaching strongly and boldly against sin and unrighteousness.

We need to rise up! To be warriors who are willing to go on the offensive and not just stay on the defensive but to stand victoriously, taking new ground for the gospel of peace - without any fear. We must submit to God and resist the devil every single day, both individually and corporately.

Empowered to Change

Following His baptism Jesus was led into the wilderness where He defeated all the onslaughts of Satan in the power of the Holy Spirit. Jesus had power from this time forward over the forces of nature, sin, sickness, demons and death - all these obeyed His orders.

> *Jesus returned to Galilee* **in the power of the Spirit,** *and news about him spread through the whole countryside.*
> *(Luke 4:14 NIV)*

Then he went to Nazareth, where he had been brought up. And on the Sabbath day he went into the Synagogue, as was his custom. And He stood up to read and said,

> **The Spirit of the Lord is on me, because he has anointed me** *to preach good news to the poor. He has sent me to proclaim freedom for the prisoners and recovery of sight for the blind, to release the oppressed, to proclaim the year of the Lord's favour.*
> *(Luke 4:18-19 NIV)*

Peter said,

You know what has happened throughout Judea, beginning in Galilee after the baptism that John preached - how **God anointed Jesus of Nazareth with the Holy Spirit and power,** *and how* **he went around doing good and healing all who were under the power of the devil, <u>because God was with him.</u>**

(Acts 10:37-38 NIV)

Remember that Jesus had never sinned. He was a sin free man, but He had to conquer the forces of Satan for us so that we through the works that He did *(the cross)*, can conquer *with* Him.

Satan is still on the loose; there are still spiritual forces of evil that need to be driven back. But *the victory has been won,* and we are on the winning side, we have been given everything necessary to move forward in Him.

Power for the People

Jesus promised power to all believers through the Holy Spirit after He had ascended.

But **you will receive power when the Holy Spirit comes on you;** *and you will be my witnesses in Jerusalem, and in all Judea and Samaria, and to the ends of the earth.*

(Acts 1:8 NIV)

He did not say, *"some of you, one or two of you, those who have specialist ministries."* No. He said *"ALL!"* We exercise this power out of our position of being adopted into God's family, with all the rights and privileges of a child of God.

Yet to all who received him, to those who believed in his name, **he gave the right to become children of God.**
(John 1:12 NIV)

However I just want to quote something thought provoking by Dr. Martyn Lloyd-Jones some years ago when he said:

"There is nothing, I am convinced, that so quenches the Spirit as the teaching which identifies the baptism of the Holy Spirit with regeneration, but it is a very commonly held teaching today, indeed it has been the popular view for many years.

They say that the baptism of the Holy Spirit is 'non-experimental,' that it happens to everybody at regeneration. So we say 'Ah-well, I am already baptised in the Holy Spirit, it happened when I was born again, it happened at my conversion; there is nothing for me to seek, I have got it all!'

Got it all? Well, if you have 'got it all,' I simply ask in the name of God why are you as you are? If you have 'got it all,' why are you so unlike those apostles, why are you unlike New Testament Christians? *[Lloyd-Jones, p280]*

Such a quotation speaks for itself, so I won't elaborate any further, however from personal experience, I can say that from the time that I received the baptism of the Holy Spirit through the laying on of hands, I knew that the power of God had came upon me. From that moment onwards I became truly *zealous* for God and wanted to be an *ACTIVE* member of His Body (Psalm 69:9).

It was as though God had suddenly become real to me and by touching me in such a real way, I knew that I had truly found Jesus and that Jesus had truly apprehended me!

> *Now when the apostles which were at Jerusalem heard that Samaria had received the Word of God, they sent unto them Peter and John: who, when they were come down, prayed for them, that they might receive the Holy Ghost:* **(For as yet he was fallen upon none of them: only they were baptized in the name of the Lord Jesus).** *Then laid they their hands on them, and they received the Holy Ghost.*
>
> *(Acts 8:14-17)*

This is exactly what happened to me, I had been simply baptised into the name of Jesus but had not yet received the Holy Spirit. However once I did receive the Holy Spirit I knew that I had received power for commission and to overcome in this life.

Such an **overwhelming experience** was the beginning of this ministry, which God led me to walk in, over a quarter of a century ago!

You too can have such a **real experience** with God that will take you forwards into a dynamic life with Him.

This is my prayer for you!

CHAPTER 12

Forgiveness
The Key to Revival

Within this last chapter of Why War, I want to speak and focus on the all-important subject of forgiveness *(including repentance).* My trigger for this was something that I came across via the Internet, a joint interview *(back in January 2013)* between Todd Bentley and the Founders of the God Channel, Rory and Wendy Alec.

It was totally unpredictable that I would be moved by such an interview, because I had previously been quite indifferent. However to my surprise it stirred something in me, regardless of any prior misgivings about the Lakeland revival and its controversy.

All of us as believers should be interested in what God is doing in the earth today, how He is doing it and who He is doing it through. On a personal level, I am willing to lay down any preconceived notions about anything, especially if I can see God moving. Regardless of what has gone before. I refuse to be trapped by my comfort zone, which keeps me from seeing or hearing God. If any believer/leader is more loyal to his comfort zone, than to God, he/she will always feel on the outside looking in.

I learnt early on that controversy was the **rule** rather than the **exception!** I accepted this once I realised that Jesus' ministry was never free of controversy - then or now. **The loss of reputation is not rare to the ministry nor is being misunderstood or misrepresented, it comes with the territory.**

However there is a spiritual law that cannot be revoked, anymore than gravity can and that is the law of forgiveness. Scripture is absolute when it comes to forgiveness. IF we forgive, THEN we are forgiven. It's that simple but no one said it was easy! Nonetheless, forgiveness can be likened to a spiritual key that unlocks spiritual doors and opportunities! *"He who opens and no one shuts, and shuts and no one opens"* (Revelation 3:7 NKJV). Or as one other translation puts it: *"The One who possesses the key of David, which **opens the*** *possibilities so that no one can shut them. The One who **closes all options** so that no one can open"* (Revelation 3:7 Voice).

When we forgive, a RELEASE takes place that can catapult us into our future and our destiny. But vice versa is also true. **All of us remain in bondage when we refuse to forgive.** We self injure and self-destruct when we choose not to forgive.

After Lakeland, most folks could not hear of Todd Bentley anymore, his marriage, tattoos or anything else for that matter because they felt letdown or betrayed! Putting such things aside, **I found myself being moved by the Spirit after seeing Todd, Rory and Wendy openly discuss, repent and forgive one another before the entire Body of Christ during that interview.**

The "conviction" that I was left with was that God was definitely in that interview and was doing something new with them all, including the God TV family. I sensed a new day had come to the Body of Christ. FORGIVENESS ALWAYS PRECEDES OUR NEXT LEVEL.

Unless You Release others You won't be Released

Forgive, and you will be forgiven.

(Luke 6:37 NIV)

Such repentance will affect a lot of people globally and usher in a new revival. Consequently Todd Bentley moved on after that and was used in revival once again, in Pretoria and Johannesburg South Africa. God certainly moved. Plus Todd had an added maturity and wisdom!

In the same way we too can experience a personal revival in all that God has promised for us, as words that have brought curses are broken. We must never underestimate the significance of forgiveness. There is a release of power when forgiveness takes place, both corporately and individually.

On the other hand precious people all over the world, remain in bondage today, **because of the words of their own mouths,** spoken negatively over themselves or others. The truth is they will never experience personal revival, all the while they are not willing to forgive.

In his book "The Secret Kingdom" Pat Robertson wrote about the Law of Reciprocity:

"One simple declaration by Jesus revealed a law that will change the world: *'Give, and it will be given to you'* (Luke 6:38 NASB). **Eight words, they form a spiritual principle that touches every relationship, every condition of man, whether spiritual or physical.** They are pivotal in any hope we have… Jesus expanded the universality of this theme throughout His ministry, varying subject matter and application. His point was so encompassing that it demanded many illustrations. In the discourse from which we get the eight words, we find this expansion: 'just as you want people to treat you, treat them in the same way' (Luke 6:31 NASB). And from that, of course, came what the world describes as the **GOLDEN RULE: 'Do unto others as you would have them do unto you.'**

Jesus went on, putting a frame around the eight key words in this manner:

Be merciful, just as your Father is merciful. And do not pass judgement and you shall not be judged: and you will be pardoned. Give, and it will be given to you; good measure, pressed down, shaken together, running over, they will pour into your lap, For whatever measure you deal out to others, it will be dealt to you in return.

(Luke 6:36-38 NASB)

By putting this together with the world's greatest teaching on love, repeated from the Old Testament by Jesus as the heart of God's will, we establish the perfect "law" for conduct: *'YOU SHALL LOVE YOUR NEIGHBOUR AS YOURSELF'* (Matthew 22:39 NASB)" *[Robertson, p113-114].*

The Anointing flows Down not Up!

It was in 2008 that the Lakeland revival collapsed and a genuine RESTORATION process began. Then five years later we saw a public show of humility between Todd Bentley, Rory and Wendy Alec. They openly discussed repentance and forgiveness, between them and the entire Body of Christ - that interview was a good example to set before us all.

Leaders are obligated to lead by example and from personal experience I can verify just how effective such a time of open repentance and forgiveness can help - to lift spiritual blockades that develop over time - due to sin, division, hurts, burn-out, wrong heart motives and more.

God can't move anywhere, if there is sin in the camp *(where there is no repentance)* or unforgiveness at the helm. *"Precious OIL POURED ON THE HEAD RUNNING DOWN on the beard, RUNNING DOWN on Aaron's beard, DOWN on the collar of his robe"* (Psalm 133:2 NIV).

NOTICE HOW THE ANOINTING RUNS "DOWN" NOT UP! The same is true for the Church. The anointing is first poured on the HEAD. This denotes Christ, but also leadership, then to the rest of the Body. So if the leadership does not have their acts together, so that the anointing can flow, this will cut off the flow for the rest of the Body.

In vice-versa, if those in leadership are right with God, then everyone else benefits from the anointing that flows down. It can never be the laypeople's fault that the anointing is not flowing as it should. The responsibility rests with the leadership. NEEDLESS TO SAY, WHEN LEADERS ARE RESTORED, IT'S IN THE BEST INTEREST OF EVERYONE! **WE MUST NEVER RESIST RESTORATION.**

Anyhow following this interview *(January 2013)* I found myself for the rest of that day *(with the leading of the Holy Spirit)* pouring over hours of research. Going through old and new footage, listening to more interviews and much more; praying, thinking and contemplating my previous stance, and seeking God.

I concluded with a renewed sense of humility towards all that the Holy Spirit was doing in the earth, particularly through the prophetic and apostolic moves. I was fully convinced that such a mood of repentance and forgiveness was necessary for revival, and relevant for the entire Body of Christ.

So much RESTORATION is still needed, in so many different quarters, right across the board. We simply won't get by without it, corporately or individually. And for such leaders to have openly repented and globally so, *(not just in front of select viewers but the entire Body of Christ)*, was a very healthy new beginning and made way for some Latter Rain!

In other words, THE BEST IS YET TO COME! Knowing that this was not limited to what the God Channel or Todd Bentley were doing, but all about what God is doing. It just so happens that God uses such people to reach millions of souls for Christ and this end time harvest certainly needs its labourers!

The destroyer comes, but God rebukes the devourer and restoration takes place. Only the Body must not turn against its own Head *(leadership)* and refuse restoration. This would be detrimental.

The adversary capitalizes on our ignorance, which is why so many of GOD'S PEOPLE perish for the lack of knowledge. *"MY PEOPLE are DESTROYED for lack of knowledge"* (Hosea 4:6). What is the knowledge they lack? It is the knowledge of God Himself! *(His person, His agenda - what He is doing in the earth and how He is doing it)*.

> *MY PEOPLE ARE BEING <u>DESTROYED</u> BECAUSE THEY DON'T KNOW ME. SINCE YOU PRIESTS REFUSE TO KNOW <u>ME</u>, I refuse to recognize you as my priests. Since you have forgotten the laws of your God, I will forget to bless your children.*
>
> *(Hosea 4:6 NLT)*

Restoration Releases New Hope

All in all I developed a renewed respect for Rory and Wendy Alec and was not so much interested in the opinions of others at that point, as I was with knowing God's WILL on the subject! **AND HIS WILL IS ALWAYS ONE OF "RESTORATION."**

We must never lose sight of the fact that the working of the Holy Spirit includes the ministry of RECONCILIATION AND RESTORATION. In fact in many ways this is the lifeblood of the Body of Christ, without it, we cannot corporately move forwards in any real or sustainable way, regardless of what has gone-on before - we are all the wiser for it!

In a similar time frame, Benny Hinn was reunited with his ex-wife. Lots of "debate and chatter" circled around such events, *(whether approval or disapproval, judgmental or critical)* and it spread right across the global Internet like a contagious-virus!

Even so, I was and am utterly convinced that people still want to see the power of restoration in demonstration, *(despite their doubts)* because it gives them hope in their own situations. Most people would be willing to invest the time that's required in order for restoration to be fully effected, as long as full restoration took place. Restoration does take TIME. But during such TIME God can do many mighty things!

I have learnt and re-learnt in my own ministry, that when nothing seems to be happening, often that's when most is happening! Like Hosea 4 told us, we must KNOW our God. We must know how His Holy Spirit is on the job 24/7 and technically there is never a time when God is not working, moving, hovering, brooding, fixing, answering... but it is only as we trust Him that RESTORATION can take place and His perfect will fulfilled in our lives, *(see Psalm 125:1; Isaiah 40:31; Jeremiah 17:7-8; Proverbs 28:25)*.

The only people who qualify for all the promises of the bible are those who actively TRUST God everyday of their lives. WE ONLY QUALIFY IF WE HAVE A LIVING **TRUST IN GOD.**

> *I will say of the Lord, He is my refuge and my fortress, my God; on Him I lean and rely, and in Him I [confidently] trust!*
> *(Psalm 91:2 AMP)*

> *My refuge, and my bulwark, my God, I trust in Him.*
> *(Psalm 91:2 YLT)*

The message of restoration is all powerful because it totally rebuffs hopelessness, which is very important since hopelessness can cause heart-sickness; *"Hope deferred makes the heart sick"* (Proverbs 13:12). **RESTORATION SENDS OUT THE UNMISTAKABLE MESSAGE THAT GOD IS BIGGER THAN ALL THE CIRCUMSTANCES, THE OPINIONS OF MEN, ALL SPIRITUAL OPPOSITION AND HOPELESSNESS.** A message worth preaching!

We MUST therefore be willing to see people properly restored, *(with accountability and with much wisdom)*. The following scripture reveals the exact attitude that God wants us to have towards RESTORATION:

> *Brethren, if any person is overtaken in misconduct or sin of any sort, **you who are spiritual [who are responsive***

to and controlled by the Spirit] should set him right and __RESTORE__ AND REINSTATE HIM, without any sense of superiority and with all __gentleness__, keeping an attentive eye on yourself, lest you should be tempted also.

(Galatians 6:1 AMP)

Prayer

Father thank You that I can walk in forgiveness today. That I have the power to choose and I choose to treat others the same way I would want them to treat me. Through Christ I have freely received and choose to freely give. Father help me by Your Spirit this day, to walk in unbroken forgiveness, in Jesus mighty name. Amen

Confession

The law of reciprocity exists just like gravity. As I measure out to others, it's measured back to me. Mercy was given to me and is mine to give. I do that today in Jesus name.

Forward or Pass it On!

Note: If this book has blessed you, let it bless others. Share it, and let the message bear fruit in someone else's life. *"What you have heard... entrust to... others"* (2 Timothy 2:2). Why not sow by gifting a copy, or even placing a bundle in the hands of your home group or church? In this way the truth multiplies and glorifies our Heavenly Father.

A massive Thank You

❖

Bibliography

- Bragg, E.C. Systematic Theology, Pneumatology. E.C. Bragg Library at Trinity College of Florida, Trinity, Florida, USA, 1990.

- Johnston, Bill. Hosting the Presence. Published by Destiny Image® Publishers, Inc. Shippensburg, Pennsylvania, USA, 2012.

- Lloyd-Jones, Dr. Martyn. The Christian Warfare, An Exposition of Ephesians 6:10-13. Published by Banner of Truth Trust, Edinburgh, Scotland; Carlisle, Pennsylvania, USA, 1976.

- Renner, Dr. Rick. Dressed to Kill. Published by Teach All Nations, Tulsa, Oklahoma, USA, 1991/2007.

- Robertson, Pat. The Secret Kingdom. Published by World Publishing, Dallas, USA, 1992.

- Strong's, James. Exhaustive Concordance. Touch Bible™ (KJV + Strong's Concerdance), Copyright ©2011 Patrick Franklin.

- Unless otherwise indicated, all scripture quotations are from the King James Version of the bible.

- Scripture quotations marked AMP are taken from The Amplified Bible. Old Testament copyright © 1965, 1987 by Zondervan Corporation, Grand Rapids, Michigan.

Drs Alan and Jennifer Pateman

Senior and Co-Apostles

Drs Alan and Jennifer Pateman, missionaries
from the UK, who at present reside in Tuscany, Italy,
and travel together as an apostolic couple. They
are the Founders of Alan Pateman World Missions,
Connecting for Excellence International,
and LifeStyle International Christian University.
President and Vice President of
World Missions Ministries Association
and APMI Publishing/Publications.

*(Please see our website for all profile and
international information, itinerant, conferences
and graduations, etc.)*

www.AlanPatemanWorldMissions.com

❖

To Contact the Author

Please email:

Alan Pateman World Missions

Email: apostledr@alanpatemanworldmissions.com
Web: www.AlanPatemanWorldMissions.com

*Please include your prayer requests
and comments when you write.*

❖

Other Books

TONGUES, Our Supernatural Prayer Language

In writing to the church at Corinth, Paul encouraged them to continue the practice of speaking with other tongues in their worship of God and in their prayer lives as a means of spiritual edification. "He that speaketh in an unknown tongue edifies, charges, builds himself up like a battery."

ISBN: 978-1-909132-44-3, Pages: 144,
Format: Paperback, Published: 2016
Also available in eBook format!

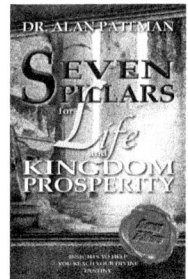

Seven Pillars for Life and Kingdom Prosperity

I submit these "Seven Pillars for Life and Kingdom Prosperity" to you, (Love, Prayer, Righteousness, Obedience, Connections, Management, Money). It's my desire that you walk in the triumphs that God has ordained for you.

ISBN: 978-1-909132-46-7, Pages: 220,
Format: Paperback, Published: 2016
Also available in eBook format!

ALAN PATEMAN WORLD MISSIONS.COM

FOR YOUR CONTINUOUS SUPPORT, WE ARE FAMILY

Patrons Benefits:

1) Patrons monthly news letter

2) Personal mentoring with Dr. Alan through WhatsApp and Prayer

3) Free Book every year

4) Teaching Courses for personal study

5) Free Conference every year

6) Free Patrons Dinner

Tel: 0039 366 329 1315

... for those who are Hungry to be Empowered

All Books Available

at

APMI PUBLICATIONS

Email: publications@alanpatemanworldmissions.com
*Also Available from Amazon.com
and other retail outlets.*

*If you purchased this book through Amazon.com
or other and enjoyed reading it, or perhaps one of
my other books, I would be grateful if you could
take a couple of minutes to write a Customer
Review, many thanks.*

BY DR. ALAN PATEMAN

The Reality of a Warrior

La Realta del Guerriero *(Italian Translation)*

Healing and Deliverance, A Present Reality

Control, A Powerful Force

His Life is in the Blood

Sexual Madness, In a Sexually Confused World *(co-authored with Jennifer Pateman)*

Apostles, Can the Church Survive Without Them?

Prayer, Ingredients for Successful Intercession, Part One

Prayer, Touching the Heart of God, Part Two

The Early Years, Anointed Generals Past and Present, Part One of Four

Revival Fires, Anointed Generals Past and Present, Part Two of Four

Why War, A Biblical Approach to the Armour of God and Spiritual Warfare

Forgiveness, the Key to Revival

His Faith, Positions us for Possession

Seduction & Control: Infiltrating Society and the Church

Kingdom Management for Anointed Prosperity

TONGUES, our Supernatural Prayer Language

Seven Pillars for Life and Kingdom Prosperity

WINNING by Mastering your Mind

Laying Foundations

Apostles and the Local Church

Preparations for Ministry

Developments and Provision

The Age of Apostolic Apostleship

Media, Spiritual Gateway *(co-authored with Jennifer Pateman)*

Israel, the Question of Ownership

Earnestly Contending for the State of Israel

The Temple, Antichrist and the New World Order

The Antichrist, Rapture and the Battle of Armageddon

Israel, the Church and the End Times

Introduction to all things APMI

Student's Handbook, Study Guide Volume 2

Empowered to Overcome

Equipped for Spiritual Warfare

Appropriations of African Territory

China, Covid-19, World Domination

Watchers of the 4 Kings

Coronavirus – Communist and Marxist Uprising

Changing Worlds, The Great Reset Deception

Davos and the Great Reset

The Ukraine Conflict – Waking Up to a New World Order

God's Anointed Well Diggers

Campus Set Up Helper, Study Guide Volume 3

Campus Guideline Handbook, Study Guide Volume 4

Instructor's Handbook, Study Guide Volume 5

The Fire of God that Gives us the Boldness to Break Free of Religion

Power or Influence

Breaking Out, Financial Freedom

God's Ways of Financial Increase

The Wonders of Christmas

Receiving Grace

Eagles of Destiny ...a Prophetic Concept

The Breakthrough is found in His Presence (31 Day Devotional)

Excellent Conduct

Kingdom Embrace

Believing in Kingdom Authority

By Your Consent

Living in His Overcoming Faith

The Culture of HONOUR

Truth for the Journey

I Need You, HOLY SPIRIT

The Apostolic Reformation and Restoration

The Nature of the Apostolic

The Triune God

The Road to Maturity

The Warrior's Garb

The Warrior's Stance

Three Faces of Control

Free to be Responsible

Fantasy Explosion for the Heavy Viewer

Breaking Free

From Bondage to Freedom

Jezebel Influencing the Church

New Age Seduction

Marriage Under Threat

The Controlling Syndrome

My Biography

The Python Spirit is Sent to Strangle our Success

The Power of Deliverance

Please, I Have a Question

Prophetic Trumpets and he that Overcomes

Kingdom Dimensions–Being Triumphant over all our Insecurities

By Dr. Jennifer Pateman

Sexual Madness, In a Sexually Confused World (co-authored with Alan Pateman)

Millennial Myopia, From a Biblical Perspective

Media, Spiritual Gateway (co-authored with Alan Pateman)

Truth Endures to All Generations

What comes first the Chicken or the Egg?

Writing Guidelines for Research Papers, Study Guide Volume 6

Writing Guidelines for Bachelor and Master Theses, Study Guide Volume 7

Writing Guidelines for Doctoral Dissertations, Study Guide Volume 8

Available from APMI Publications, Amazon.com and Other Retail Outlets

www.ingramcontent.com/pod-product-compliance
Lightning Source LLC
Chambersburg PA
CBHW071534040426
42452CB00008B/1012